FORMULA FOR FAMILY UNITY

A practical guide for Christian families

FORMULA FOR FAMILY UNITY

A practical guide for Christian families

Walter and Trudy Fremont

BOB JONES UNIVERSITY PRESS

GREENVILLE, SOUTH CAROLINA 29614

Formula for Family Unity
by Walter and Trudy Fremont

©1980 Bob Jones University Press
Greenville, South Carolina 29614

Printed in the United States of America

90 89 88 87   10 9 8 7 6

Library of Congress Cataloging-in-Publication Data

Fremont, Walter, 1924-
    Formula for family unity.

    1. Family—Religious life. 2. Family—
Biblical teaching. I. Fremont, Trudy,
1926-   . II. Title.
BV4526.2.F73   1986   248.4   86-11745
ISBN 0-89084-122-5

Preface

Many books have been written in the last few years on how to find happiness in marriage. The motivation for these books has been sparked in most cases by the tremendous upsurge in the divorce rate and the increase in troubled Christian marriages. We have seen in our counselling and weekend seminars an urgent need for a return to Bible principles that can be put into action in day-by-day family situations.

Many Christians have strange, unbiblical ideas about love, communication, submission, sex, the husband's leadership, handling children, facing crises, and a host of other concepts involved in marriage and family life. We can have Christlike actions and responses in any situation only if we know exactly how Christ wants us to act as He has revealed in His Word. Looking to the Word of God for direction and the Holy Spirit for power to carry out His Word in love is the only answer for a marriage that would honor the Lord and produce children who serve the Lord. We are grateful for many men and women who are pointing people away from psychology and back to basic Bible principles for solutions to their problems.

After hearing 30 years of daily chapel preaching and Bible Conference speaking, listening to thousands of sermons in 37 years as a Christian attending church, and reading hundreds of books on counselling and marriage, we find it difficult to identify the source of ideas or give due credit. However, with all of the input, we long ago came to the conclusion that Bible truths, when put into action, hold the key to happiness and a marriage that exalts our Lord and Saviour Jesus Christ.

In our weekend seminars, which we have been holding since 1964; classes in American family, child psychology, adolescent psychology, and child development; and "The Wilds" couples' retreats, we have received hundreds of questions that seem to fall into some predictable patterns and areas. In this book we have tried to answer important questions in each area with basic Bible concepts. This book could well be used in premarital counselling or as a help to well-established marriages that need an extra boost for happiness. Family unity is the goal. *"And if a house be divided against itself, that house cannot stand" (Mark 3:25).* Bible principles provide the formula for family unity.

When Christians get married, they form a permanent relationship that will usually last 50 to 70 years. These years can be a beautiful, pleasant pathway of happiness if the couple follows Bible Action Truths.

For the sake of ease in reading, the pronouns "he" and "his" are often used in the book to refer to both men and women.

Contents

FORMULA FOR FAMILY UNITY

A practical guide for Christian families

1 Deciding on Happiness in Marriage

Someone once quipped, "Marriage is like a besieged city; everyone on the outside is trying to get in and everyone on the inside is trying to get out." Humor can often soften life's harsh realities. However, though we may gloss over the truth, we cannot erase it. Recent statistics show that an increasing number of couples—approximately one-third—are concluding that marriage is not worth the effort.

Are Christians exempt from these growing marital problems? Unfortunately, they are not. Isaiah 53:6 reminds us that all are prone to go astray. A godly heritage does not make anyone immune to temptation, and we must face the fact that—even for Christians—a successful marriage takes work.

This is not to say, however, that believers don't have a distinct advantage over non-believers; they do, for Christians should know where to find the answers to the problems that confront them. God's Word sets forth the principles needed for guiding a marriage toward success. Let's look at three general concepts that form the basis for a scriptural outlook.

First, God is an all-wise creator. *"As for God, his way is perfect: the word of the Lord is tried: he is a buckler to all those that trust in him" (Psalm 18:30).* This verse assures us that God's wisdom is perfect and the Christian may be confident of His choice for a life partner. He makes no mistakes. God will choose, or possibly has already chosen, the person who can best meet the husband's needs and whose needs the husband can best meet. The assurance of this promise rests on a prior knowledge of God's reliability, or faithfulness. His provision for salvation and His daily protection are reminders—God cares for His children and will aid them when they ask. Consequently, if problems arise, God's child can look to Him as a "buckler." Even a mate's imperfections may be a tool to help the Christian grow toward Christlikeness (Ephesians 2:10).

Marriage is a binding union till death separates the partners. *"What God hath joined together, let not man put asunder" (Matthew 19:6).* Marriage is not only a legal contract but also a contract and vow made before God. Divorce cannot be an escape for those who know Christ. Some may ask, "Didn't Moses sanction divorce in the Old Testament?" Christ answered this question in Matthew's Gospel. He restricted the Mosaic law by specifying that adultery was the only basis for divorce (Matthew 19:8, 9). This passage does not imply that adultery necessitates divorce. Forgiveness, though difficult, is the preferred route. Christ explained that the Israelites' hard hearts motivated Moses's sanction.

This point brings us to another question. What if divorce has already taken place? If such is the case and the Christian has not yet remarried, according to Scripture he does not have the freedom to do so. Though he is legally free from his former spouse, God says that he may remarry only if his former spouse dies (Romans 7:1-3, I Corinthians 7:11, 15 and 39). If, however, a remarriage has already occurred, there is no way to right the wrong (Luke 16:17, 18). The Christian must ask forgiveness and rely on God to make his second marriage successful. He must also realize that certain avenues of service are now closed to him (I Timothy 3:2-11); nonetheless, it is God's will that he honor his present contract.

Happiness is the believer's responsibility. Abraham Lincoln said, "Most folks are about as happy as they make up their minds to be." He was right. The Christian couple must strive daily to create experiences that will enhance their marriage and solve the irritations that arise. To do so they must realize that problems need a cooperative, not a condemning, attitude. As they arise, family problems should not be exaggerated or ignored. Exaggerating a problem will destroy communication, and ignoring it will cause bad feelings to fester. When something is wrong in the house, the owner doesn't burn the house down; he fixes what is wrong. The same principle holds true in a marriage. When something is wrong, Christians talk it over and solve the problem; they do not threaten divorce.

These three principles may be helpful in problem-solving. First of all, the Christian attacks the problem—not the person. Second, he keeps things in their proper perspective and doesn't make mountains out of molehills. (The forgotten matches at a family picnic should not cause a blow-up. The car lighter will start the fire just as effectively.) Third, he takes one day at a time. When a problem arises, he deals with it specifically. He doesn't remind his partner that she may have irritated him yesterday, nor does he wave past mistakes in front of her. Instead, he tries to turn these potentially problematic situations into a happy time by utilizing his creativity. (For example, a wrong turn on a vacation jaunt can be the start of a new adventure. The creative person concentrates on what he can see and learn from this mistake rather than on the few minutes lost.)

Today, car accidents, heart attacks, and various other tragedies claim the lives of thousands of people daily. It would help all Christians to remember that God has blessed them greatly by allowing them to enjoy the company of those they love. Because the Christian does not know what God has for him in the future, he should live each day with his loved ones as if it were the last.

2 The Participant's Character

It is one thing to understand the concepts of a successful marriage, but it is quite another matter to put these principles into practice. The success or failure of the marriage union depends largely upon the character of those united.

Everyone has a basic set of values or beliefs. In essence there are only two systems to choose from—the biblical or the worldly. The basic difference between these two systems is that the biblical standard seeks to please God while the worldly standard seeks to please self. The worldly standard is feeling-oriented, but the biblical standard is guided by absolute principles—those prinples found in God's Word.

A Christian with strong character acts consistently upon biblical principle; conversely, a Christian with weak character wavers between a biblical and worldly standard. Some unsaved people act upon a worldly, self-centered plane all of the time, while others of weaker character are more feeling-oriented and vacillate between "moral" and selfish behavior, depending on their mood.

God's Word tells us that "light and darkness" are incompatible. Therefore, the union of the saved and the unsaved will not work. A man unable to control his temper, who beats his wife and neglects his children, probably not only has weak character but also needs to be saved. So also a woman who is rebellious, stubborn, and deceitful (one who uses various psychological methods to gain selfish ends) needs salvation. Until both husband and wife take this initial step of salvation, a good marriage will be very difficult—if not impossible. *"Wherefore he saith, Awake thou that sleepest, and arise from the dead, and Christ shall give thee light" (Ephesians 5:14).*

A Christian needs to be cautioned, however, against union with the unsaved, but he also needs to make certain that once he has accepted Christ he and his spouse grow toward spiritual maturity, for a person of weak character will also be a vacillating marriage partner.

Ephesians 5:15-19 mentions four steps toward developing a strong Christian character.

Walking circumspectly. *"See then that ye walk circumspectly, not as fools, but as wise" (Ephesians 5:15).* Both mental attitude and desires change after a person is saved. He becomes aware of the fallacies of the world's system, such as, today's mania of governmental control. The government is trying to purify our environment and food. Their apparent motivation is society's "physical well-being," but despite their great interest in our "well-being," they permit the sale of liquor and subsidize tobacco. It is easy for a Christian to see that the motivation of these people is not entirely altruistic.

Thus, once a person is saved, not only his perspective but his actions change. He begins to act upon biblical principles. He no longer seeks to gratify self, but seeks rather to please God. His love for God motivates him to love others and to seek their welfare as well as his own. Thus, "walking circumspectly" and obeying God's Word enables a Christian to be a loving, wise marriage partner.

Redeeming the time. It is also imperative that a Christian be *"redeeming the time because the days are evil"* *(Ephesians 5:16).* Redeeming the time involves using the Scripture to evaluate surroundings and to properly order priorities. Prayer, Bible reading, and daily obedience to the Bible will increase a Christian's ability to fulfill his responsibility to redeem the time. But he also needs to get his priorities in line with God's Word, for a balanced Christian life is one of four priorities: God, spouse, children, and ministry.

Christ should be first on any Christian's list of priorities. Obedience to Him is the first responsibility. The next major concern is the marriage partner. Every marriage should be a picture of Christ and His bride. Since this symbolic thread is woven throughout the Old and New Testaments, it is obvious that Christ holds marriage in high esteem. If Christians give Christ the preeminence, then this analogy will follow in their lives.

One of the most precious gifts of marriage is children, the Christian's third priority. If parents fail to govern them properly, these children will mar the parents' testimony. The unsaved will not listen to their "formula" for successful living if their children reject their message.

The final major responsibility is a Christian's

God-given ministry. If the first three priorities are well taken care of, God can then bless the fourth. Redeeming the time necessitates that certain duties take precedence over others. Overcommitment is the weakness of many zealous Christian workers. They let the good become the enemy of the best. Some may know God has called them to a particular ministry in a church, but they let five other jobs in the church take up all their time. Their real ministry suffers and does not grow. The five other jobs get a "lick and a promise," and the family gets little or no attention. A Christian's looking to God's Word and the Holy Spirit's leadership will establish the priorities that insure a balanced Christian life.

Being filled with the Spirit of God. *"Wherefore be ye not unwise, but understanding what the will of the Lord is. And be not drunk with wine, wherein is excess; but be filled with the Spirit" (Ephesians 5:17, 18).* Drinking wine changes a person's behavior temporarily. God, however, wants a positive, permanent change, and He has provided the prescription for it: the filling of the Holy Spirit. Through the Scripture the Holy Spirit can direct our lives.

Much is being said about the infilling of the Holy Spirit. Despite this fact, however, few Christians understand the principle. They realize that the Spirit comes into their lives when they are saved (Romans 8:9), but they do not know how to be filled. Scripture gives two simple steps to follow. First, confess all known sin; then yield completely to the Holy Spirit.

The first step is easily understood, but the second one is often confusing. "Yielding" is not a one-time dedication at a special revival or campfire meeting. It is a daily submission of the will to God. Real surrender means, "I am going to yield my will and body each moment to Christ; it will not be my desires today but God's" (Galatians 2:20 and Luke 9:23).

Not long ago, I was talking to a pastor who told me of his wife's method of daily renewing her dedication. He said, "She is a singing Christian in the morning. She gets up happily—she literally begins the day rejoicing. Then she steps before the mirror, and the first thing she says is 'drop dead.'" This is her way of reminding herself that she is *"dead to sin and yielded to righteousness"* (Romans 6:11, 12, 13).

Praising God. *"Speaking to yourselves in psalms and hymns and spiritual songs, singing and making melody in your heart to the Lord; giving thanks always for all things unto God and the Father in the name of our Lord Jesus Christ"* (Ephesians 5:19-20). Verses 19 and 20 are natural outgrowths of the previous steps. Once the mind and heart has been transformed to the image of Christ by the filling of the Spirit, praise is a natural, spontaneous reaction.

The steps toward building a strong, Christian character are simple to follow and essential for success. Once these principles are put into practice, marriage problems as well as life's other problems will fall into their proper perspective. Two people who have yielded their soul, mind, and heart to God can have a truly joy-filled Christian marriage.

CASE STUDY

A mother called me and asked me to help her 26-year-old son and daughter-in-law whose marriage was breaking up. Both the husband

and wife were eager for help and came from a town 20 miles away to see me the next day. He had hair down to his shoulders, and her dress revealed more than it covered. They had been married for seven years, had two children, a new home, and a good income, but they were not happy.

The husband admitted, "We have everything that anyone could want, and we have tried everything that could give us happiness, including regular use of pot, but we just aren't happy. We have searched for happiness, but even though we now have everything we've ever dreamed about, we are still frustrated." He did find a certain amount of enjoyment in hunting, but as he said, "That doesn't increase the unity in our marriage, and even though I enjoy it, I still feel that it's useless." His wife was becoming very fearful, nervous, and continually dissatisfied.

They had both come from a religious background but had generally rejected their heritage in their quest for fun and excitement. I talked with them about the problem of sin and selfishness in their lives and showed them from the Scripture how they could receive Christ as their personal Saviour to gain complete forgiveness and satisfy the terrible longing of their souls. They both accepted Christ that day, and many changes began to take place in their lives almost immediately, including a new-found unity in their marriage.

I visited them once a week to help them grow in their new faith. A two-pack-a-day cigarette habit concerned both of them for about three months until they gained victory over it. They also decided to attend a weekend couples' retreat at a nearby camp, "The Wilds." This altered their lives for it was at this camp that they dedicated themselves to full-time service. Deciding to live a crucified life, they sold their home, moved to Greenville, South Carolina, and he entered Bob Jones University as a ministerial student.

Salvation and the filling of the Holy Spirit drastically changed these two young people's lives. It has brought them love and unity in their marriage and given them a purpose for living and a sense of fulfillment. In their case these two steps provided the keys to the abundant life. They now feel led to the mission field and are following God's direction for their lives.

3 How to Love—A Mental Attitude

"I don't think my husband loves me. He never pays any attention to me. He's away from home most of the time, works an extra part-time job, and then, when he is off on Sunday, he sleeps all day. He doesn't even go to church anymore. The first two years of our marriage were fine, but in the last three years things have been getting worse and worse. I don't even know if I love him anymore. Maybe I married the wrong man." Does this story sound familiar? This is the attitude of a person who does not know the true meaning of love.

All will surely agree that love is an important ingredient in a successful marriage. By understanding the true meaning of love, Christians can see beyond the attitude that prevails today.

Hollywood and popular music promote the myth that love is a mere feeling. However, Scripture says that love is not a feeling but a mental attitude that prevails despite illness, heartache, and financial difficulties. As a matter of fact, unpleasant circumstances often provide opportunity for real love to grow. Real love, then, is "an unselfish or self-sacrificing desire to meet the needs of the cherished object." Though this definition is neither poetic nor romantic, it is accurate.

The key theme of love is "meeting needs." The Christian can choose to love any cherished object; and, loving it, he will determine what the cherished object's needs are and how he can meet them. For example, a man may love his car. If he does, he will spend time waxing it, tuning it, and buying gadgets to dress it up. He will give both time and money toward its maintenance.

On a more elevated plane, love for God also fits this definition. One who loves God will attempt to understand and meet His needs. Of course, Acts 17:25 indicates that God, in reality, needs nothing from men; but He asks certain things of them, desiring their good. He asks obedience (John 14:21). He desires praise and worship (Psalm 107:8), and He bids men fellowship with Him (John 1:7-9). If a man truly loves God he will respond to His commands and requests.

The same principle applies to married love. In O.Henry's "Gift of the Magi," the poor man sold his watch to buy combs for his wife's hair, and she sold her beautiful long hair to buy a chain for his watch. Though each of their gifts had lost any extrinsic value by the time it was received, the motivation behind the giving made the gift precious. Both the husband and wife had demonstrated their love.

In order to utilize these established principles, the Christian must first understand his partner's needs. God has created man and woman to complement each other by supplying differing needs: emotional, intellectual, and physical.

A WOMAN'S NEEDS

Security is one of the two basic desires of a woman. Most women recognize this psychological need in themselves, and a good husband will also. Being consistently supportive, being present at crucial times and acting wisely in solving various family problems are all ways in which a good husband can meet his wife's need for security. Every Christian husband should glean his strength from Christ and then strive to point his family toward this same rock of security.

The husband must also seek to exhibit his love and give security through communication. He should talk with his wife daily. This verbal communication is even more important than the physical communication for women. Women need a time to sit down and converse about simple, everyday matters. Although such conversation seems unimportant to the wheeling-and-dealing executive-husband, it is imperative for maintaining a sympathetic understanding in marriage.

A good husband will also be careful not to make his wife jealous or give her any reason to question his love. In addition, men and women who are innately jealous or who lacked love as children need a double dose of affection.

It is tragic to see a man who would rather be mothered than meet his family's needs, for both the wife and children become very insecure in this situation. A good husband will seek to fulfill his responsibilities rather than insist on being pampered constantly.

A woman's second basic need, the homemaking need, is interwoven with the desire for having chil-

dren and providing those children with a good environment. A woman needs knick-knacks, bric-a-brac, dust-catchers, and all kinds of dainty things to make her "house" a "home." Her negligence in housekeeping is one sign that her needs are not being met. Consequently, a sensitive husband will do all he can to keep the house well maintained. A good coat of paint in the kitchen can do wonders since a wife spends most of her time there; and although the man controls the budget, he should allot his wife a certain amount yearly to spend as she wishes on the home. Nagging cannot change a woman's slovenly housekeeping habits, but keeping the house in good condition will go a long way toward changing her.

A MAN'S NEEDS

Many a woman wants to change her husband after the marriage, but this desire can only lead to problems. She may complain that he spits in the sink, throws his clothes on the floor, or leaves his shoes by the TV every night. She feels that he needs to change these bad habits, but the wise woman doesn't say a word. Instead, she praises the Lord that her husband doesn't chew tobacco; then she concentrates first on turning chores like picking up his clothes and shoes into labors of love and second on meeting his needs.

Man's first need involves his ego. A wise woman will never tear down her husband, either in private or public. The coffee-clatch chats about "that terrible husband of mine" are very dangerous. Even subtle nagging at home tears down a husband's ego.

A wise wife will build her husband up before the children and others. Comments such as "We have the best daddy; we are so proud of you; you're a wonderful lover" all go a long way in cementing the love relationship. A true helpmate encourages her husband and builds his confidence.

Man's second basic need is his physical need— both for food and love. The old adage, "The best way to a man's heart is through his stomach," is a true saying. Never bring up problems before supper. A man can become very nervous, jumpy, and irritable when he is hungry.

A loving wife will also meet her husband's physical need for love—she will not refuse him. Problems arise in a marriage when the partners think in terms of their own needs rather than the needs of the other. Though a woman may not have such strong physical needs as a man, she should remember that one of her husband's basic needs is physical love.

Realizing the differing needs of a partner and giving to fulfill those needs alleviates many problems. However, unselfish giving has no thought of return. II Corinthians 9:6-8 reminds us that those who sow sparingly shall reap sparingly, but those who sow bountifully shall reap bountifully as well.

The big question often accompanying the realization of this principle is "who is going to start the giving?" As one counselor says, "Too many marriages have a relationship like a tick on a dog. And in some marriages there are two ticks and no dog." Man can give without loving, but he cannot love without giving. One woman said, "I started giving

for a week, but it didn't work; he didn't respond."
I told her, "If you've been acting selfishly for nine
years, it may take five or six weeks before your
husband will respond." One can expect a time of
insecurity, a time of testing, while a partner
evaluates whether the change is genuine or whether
he is just using it as a temporary gimmick to get his
own way. Verse 7 directs the Christian to make up
his mind to love, not grudgingly or of necessity, for
God loveth a cheerful giver. He must make up his
mind to sacrifice unselfishly of time, money, and
energy in all kinds of everyday situations.

Some may argue that their partners are so hate-
ful they simply cannot put this principle into practice. But Scripture says, *"God is able to make all grace
abound toward you: that ye, always having all sufficiency in all
things, may abound to every good work" (II Corinthians 9:8).*
God's power is available to every Christian who asks
Him for strength when his partner criticizes or re-
jects him, then asks Him for the ability to love even
when indifference, neglect, and coldness are part of
the daily scene. He will help in these common situations as well as in the more difficult circumstances
of drunkenness, sadism, perversion, and other
forms of corruption. A Christian only complicates
the problems by an unloving reaction and makes the
partner's problems his problems.

For the Christian couple, married love should be
the basis for all other facets of love. If both are right
with the Lord, they will experience a bond of unity.
They will set their affections on the cherished one
and determine that they will do all in their power to
meet the other's needs.

CASE STUDY

Several years ago a ministerial student came to my office seeking help for his 11-year-old son, who had psychological problems. I asked him the usual question, "How are you and your wife getting along?"

The man answered with an explosive "Terrible! I'm thinking about leaving her."

I said, "If you do that, it will wreck your ministry."

He then blurted out a list of her faults, including stubbornness, violent temper, and physical rejection for months at a time. He said she also stayed away from church and failed to do decent housework. He admitted that he had gotten so exasperated with her that he had spanked her a few times, only making things worse.

Originally, he had left a thriving business to study for the ministry. Now he was at the point of wrecking everything by leaving his wife. We turned to II Corinthians 9:6-8, and I explained to him the principle of giving. I finished with verse 7 and emphasized that he must make up his mind to give. He stopped me, saying, "You don't understand; she is a witch." He again reiterated her faults for me. I explained verse 8 and suggested that he ask God for the grace he needed to start carrying out God's command to love his wife. I went over the seven ways that women want to be loved (explained in Chapter 7), then we prayed for God's help for him. Three weeks later I received the following letter:

"I have been by to see you in your office several times, but each time you were busy. Since so much time has elapsed since you talked to me, I feel I must write this long past due note.

"Praise God for His promises and the truth of His Word. The promise that you called to my attention and I claimed there in your office brought almost unbelievable results. I went home from the office and did exactly as you instructed me that day, and the results were immediate, though reluctant at first. We are enjoying, I believe, a home situation now that is normal for the school and work schedule that we all have to have. The violent arguments have ceased, and by the grace of God will not resume. We have been able to sit down and talk about problems more freely than ever. Another reward that this brought was a better attitude on the part of my son (eleven years).

"We now go visiting on Saturdays, health permitting, and this has helped my wife's attitude also. After all, this is what she is called to do as well as I. Thank God for a school and a faculty who are so equipped with His wisdom that this kind of help is available to those of us who desperately need it. I can, as you said, say now with conviction that I know this principle works. Again, thank you."

They are now enjoying a happy marriage in a successful ministry.

4 Communication—
The Basis for Real Love

As counselors we are often asked to determine the basic causes for the increasing divorce rate. Finances, sex problems, problem children, and in-laws are only a few of the supposed monkey wrenches that jam up the marriage gears. We have found, however, that the basic cause is a breakdown in communication.

Two Christians can solve any difference if they are willing to talk things over and arrive at an acceptable solution. They may merely agree to disagree, but at least communicating will prevent the problem from festering and ultimately creating bitterness, malice, and in some cases even hatred.

We have noticed that some people are so busy reaching for their own personal plans and goals that they don't make time for important daily communication. Good relationships are vital in welding a family together. They are more important than a clean house or a neat lawn, and it will do a wife well to remember this principle when her husband tracks mud on her new beige carpet. It is easier to clean the carpet than to repair a damaged relationship.

At a recent couples' retreat, one man came to me with this confession, "For years I've gotten furious with my wife for being late—even a few minutes late. However, today it all came to a head. We'd had a beautifully harmonious start this morning, but I ruined it all. I began railing at her because she had made me a few minutes late for flag raising. I'd even thought about not going, for it was an optional function, but once I had made up my mind to go, I became unreasonable." This man realized his problem and decided to remedy the situation by changing his habitual response and alleviating his bitter feelings. His wife was overjoyed for this new determination; for his previous responses had spoiled many happy times.

No one can deny that sharing living arrangements has its own brand of upsets. Married couples face many "unique" irritations, such as how the toilet paper is put on the holder. Some people prefer that the paper roll off the holder in front; others prefer it to roll off from the back. Failure to agree on "which technique is correct" may cause considerable irritation.

A friend of ours heard us use this illustration at one of our seminars. When she got home, she related the story to her husband. She ended her narration by saying, "Isn't it funny that people argue over such a stupid incidental?"

His reply was, "I don't think it's funny at all. You've been putting it on wrong all these years, and I've had to change it every time." They then began to argue over "who was correct." Realizing what was happening, they both began to laugh. Before the subject was closed, she agreed to put it on the "right" way in the future.

The desire for one partner to prove constantly that he or she is right indicates an insecure and divisive spirit. If this attitude persists, it may destroy a marital relationship. Each must learn to give, and to give out of a joyful heart. When problems do arise, and they are sure to, talking them over reasonably and maturely will prevent future, more severe upsets.

As we have already pointed out, men and women think differently; thus, they react differently. Scientists have observed differences even in early childhood and infancy that would validate this claim. These distinctions are too flagrant to be attributed to environment. Although some of these early characteristics are innate, others are acquired, and many of them are carried over into adulthood. Some of these are particularly consistent.

Women tend to be subtle and to hint. Men are more blunt and direct. This principle was pointed out to me one noontime as my wife and I were riding in the car. When we neared Textile Hall, where a craft show was being held, she commented, "I understand that the Hall is pretty crowded at night, but at noon it's not so much so." I continued the drive and passed the street to turn off to the Hall. "Don't you want to go?" she inquired.

"Go where?" I replied.

She said, "What in the world do you think I've been talking about?"

My response was, "Let's go, now that I know what you want."

Though a man thinks of anniversary and birth dates as trivial details, a woman will remember them and consider this remembrance very important.

Women are also more verbal. Men are slower to put things into words and will usually not bother talking unless they have full attention. This is one point a woman needs to be careful to remember and not interrupt her husband or finish his sentences for him.

It is also important that men keep in mind that women are more romantic and idealistic. They enjoy involving themselves at the feeling level (candles, perfume, and music are examples of these characteristics). Men tend to be more realistic, more action oriented (food and love without the extras).

Women are usually schedule-oriented, whereas men are more pragmatic and flexible in their planning.

Women often ramble in their explanations. They enjoy accentuating details and inconsequentials. Men are more often logical and concise in relating their ideas.

Because of natural hormone cycles, women are more periodically depressed than men. Consequently, they vacillate more in their moods; they are less predictable in their behavior than men.

Men are at times loud, brash, and gauche. Women, however, are more gentle and refined. Thus, men may tend to have more temper outbursts when frustrated.

The above traits do not *all* apply to *all* men and women. Generally, however, these are typical characteristics of each sex, and it may be helpful to remember these differences when upsetting situations arise. We tend to equate equality with sameness. Men and women are equal before God, but they were made very differently by God to fulfill their unique and complementary roles in God's perfect plan.

A number of years ago, Jay Adams, author of *Competent to Counsel*, brought to my attention several valuable rules of communication. They are based on Ephesians 4:22-32. Verses 22 through 24 admonish us to *"Put off concerning the former conversation the old man, which is corrupt according to the deceitful lusts: and be renewed in the spirit of your mind; and that ye put on the new man, which after God is created in righteousness and true holiness."*

The word *conversation* is an Old English word meaning "manner of life or behavior." Since most behavior toward a spouse is verbal, husbands and wives should concentrate on improving verbal responses. Verse 23 emphasizes the necessity of making up the mind to change. Christians are to rid themselves of corrupt behavior and start behaving God's way.

Ephesians 4:25-32 provides specific rules for good communication.

"Wherefore putting away lying, speak every man truth with his neighbour: for we are members one of another." Openness and truthfulness are the bases of Christian communication. A person should be willing to discuss all subjects with his partner and not hide feelings. Honestly stating that one is angry, disturbed, or feeling put down is a giant step toward clearing the air.

Couples also must be interested in one another's work, ideas, and opinions. They should ask questions and listen to one another, not necessarily interjecting personal ideas; for the art of conversation is the ability to ask the proper questions about topics which concern the other person—topics about which he feels qualified and informed—then to *listen* to what the other has to say. Reading the *Reader's Digest*, the newspaper, and other informative sources will aid a wife in keeping up with the current issues and events that interest her husband in his world of business. Interesting, stimulating conversation with a husband is built on more than comments about the baby's runny nose or the latest soap opera tragedy. Really listening and commenting appropriately keeps communication flowing.

"Be ye angry, and sin not: let not the sun go down upon your wrath: neither give place to the devil" (Ephesians 4:26). Anger short-circuits good communication. Anger, like love, thrives on expression and response; therefore, Christians should be careful about unrestrained expression. Feelings of mild opposition or irritation may become more intense when they are emotionally expressed. A Christian should first analyze the immediate reason for the irritation, then verbalize this reason rather than the feeling involved. Instead of saying, "I'm sick and tired of hearing about your mother," he says instead, "Your mother called again and wants us to send her a fifty dollar check; I don't think we can afford it." If, however, anger does arise, a couple should agree to table the discussion until the anger subsides.

Timing is important! Wise couples don't discuss important matters when tired, hot, or hungry. Also, they don't over-react by screaming, yelling, or crying. A man must feel secure in talking with his wife. She should refrain from retreating to the refrigerator or he from jumping into a car for an aggressive ride.

Neither should blow up or clam up—they should talk up instead.

It is also imperative to stick to the topic when solving a problem. The big mistake ten years ago or another issue has no part in today's difficulties. The following letter was printed in a local newspaper: "I've been married 17 years to a man who is good to me and the kids, but he's always been the quiet type until we have an argument. . . . For instance the other night we had an argument about the bills. . . . After he yelled about that for awhile he said, 'And another thing, why do you make fish all the time? You know I hate fish.' I was shocked. I never knew he didn't like fish. He always ate it without a word." Scripture also admonishes to dispose of anger and heal the breach *before* going to bed; *"let not the sun go down upon your wrath."* Praying together nightly and going to sleep holding hands is an ideal way to end a day.

The third rule of communication is an admonition to be industrious—to take full responsibility for one's share of the work. Verse 28 of Ephesians 4 states, *"Let him that stole, steal no more: but rather let him labour, working with his hands the thing which is good, that he may have to give to him that needeth."* Stealing someone else's time by shirking responsibilities causes anger and interrupts good communication. Men tend to be lazy around the house. A few years ago, a study of husbands of working wives revealed that the husbands helped their wives an average of 1½ hours a week, but helped so reluctantly that they made the wives feel guilty. These wives had an average of 27 hours of household chores a week beyond their normal 40-hour working week. Men often fail to realize all the work their wives do continually—cleaning, cooking, taking care of the children, and other numerous tasks. A good husband will assist his wife during times of extra burden and will encourage the children to help by doing regular chores. In this way he can ease some of the family work load, especially during holidays and times of entertaining. The wife, if aided in this way, will then have more time for daily rest and conversation.

Ephesians 4:29 states, *"Let no corrupt communication proceed out of your mouth, but that which is good to the use of edifying, that it may minister grace unto the hearers."* What one says, how he says things, and the gestures and facial expressions he uses determine whether his communication is corrupt or edifying.

There are several ways to communicate an idea. For example, I can call a person "level-headed" or "flat-headed," or "thrifty" or "stingy," but the terms I use will determine the effect of my communication. I can also say, "You have a face that would stop a clock." But it would be better to say, "When I look into your face, time stands still."

People who are hard-pressed for something nice to say should try sticking to general expressions rather than specific statements. For example, when viewing an ugly baby, a person may exclaim, "What a baby!" and be making a gracious exclamation.

Most important, each Christian is responsible for the effect of his conversation. Jokes, expressions, and general conversation should be mentally tested before being blurted out. (Let me insert here that ethnic jokes are never in good taste for the Christian.) A Christian must consider what will edify and administer grace, for he can never hide behind the lame excuse, "How did I know he would take it that way?" However, the receivers of corrupt communication have a responsibility to take it with grace and not react carnally. We must never let other peoples' problems become our problems.

Voice inflection and intensity also convey meaning. "I love you" can be said lovingly, sarcastically, harshly, angrily, helplessly, or any number of other ways. The voice can convey sincerity and truth or hypocrisy and falsehood. Men need to be particularly careful that their gruff, aggressive voices don't give children the wrong impression. All parents need to be cautioned that children are quick to pick up vocal insinuations or impatience or irritation.

Gestures and facial expressions also play an important part in conveying meaning. Christian parents need to develop the habit of smiling and nodding approvingly toward their children and spouse. Too often a critical, negative, scowling expression or stance may say more than words. Gestures should be generally open, accepting gestures, rather than closed (crossing arms) or rejecting ones (hands on hips).

In conversation a positive attitude is much more effective than a negative, critical spirit. Nagging never edifies, and trying to change a spouse by nagging will be futile. Couples marry to love, not change or remake. Thus, it is not productive to nag about irritating habits or mannerisms. Mature people can discuss such matters, but not all people are mature. If one spouse is unable to handle the discussion, it should be dropped. A Christian must keep a positive faith attitude and be sensitive about how he will affect others by what he says.

Verses 30-32 of Ephesians four give us the fifth principle on communication. *"And grieve not the holy Spirit of God, whereby ye are sealed unto the day of redemption. Let all bitterness, and wrath, and anger, and clamour, and evil speaking, be put away from you, with all malice: And be ye kind one to another, tenderhearted, forgiving one another, even as God for Christ's sake hath forgiven you."*

When a partner is wronged, a genuine "I'm sorry" from one or a sincere "I forgive you" from the other is all that is needed to clear the lines of communication. Bitterness between mates grieves the Holy Spirit and damages the relationship. If allowed to fester, it can cause a breach that may even affect the physical relationship.

Another caution is that bitterness soon develops into hatred. Hebrews 12:15 warns us, *"Looking diligently lest any man fail of the grace of God; lest any root of bitterness springing up trouble you and thereby many be defiled."* One gospel worker's wife was very bitter when she came to me. She had prepared a long written list of complaints about her spouse, dating back to 19 years before. Some of the incidents even occurred on their honeymoon. I told her that the very fact that she had kept a written record indicated a bitter, unforgiving spirit. I suggested, "Let's tear up this list and ask God to forgive you for your sin of bitterness." Her immediate reply was, "I'll ask for forgiveness, but don't tear up the list; I don't have another copy." She finally realized her problem and took care of it because complete forgiveness means forgetting and never reminding a spouse of the incident. Remembering someone's past mistakes is a sure sign that there has not been a Christlike forgiveness.

Studies on marital desires, indicating that the wife ranks companionship number one, whereas the husband ranks it number three, validate the importance of good communication in the marriage. Everyone struggles with the feeling of loneliness and the fear of rejection, but these feelings are increased in marriage when one spouse leaves the other out of his thoughts and feelings. Companionship based on Christian communication will alleviate some of these negative feelings and enhance the unity and oneness of the marital relationship.

Striving for this unity with a spouse by proper communication—speaking the truth in love—will thus promote harmony in the family. In the marriage relationship, this sharing of a life with another can be especially intimate and rewarding.

CASE STUDY

A preacher called me from out of state asking me if I would be willing to counsel his wife. He had told me that she was ready to have a nervous breakdown, and when she finally called a week later, I found out why. She told me that she had been terribly depressed for the last year and a half and that she had thought about suicide. Lately, she had become very nervous, and she was afraid that she was going to go "berserk." "It all started," she said, "when my husband made his great confession to me."

Apparently a year and a half ago he had attended a seminar in which he was instructed to confess all to anyone he had ever wronged (a very questionable suggestion). He went home and told his wife about two affairs he had had within the first year of their marriage.

After the second affair he had gotten saved and was later called to preach. He attended six years of college and seminary, had taken a church, and had had a fruitful ministry before he attended the seminar that prompted his confession. His wife admitted, "The confession may have cleared his conscience, but it has wrecked me, and it's going to wreck our marriage." She also admitted that since the day of the confession she couldn't stand for her husband to touch her, and she rarely spoke to him.

Her basic problem was evident—she was disregarding Ephesians 4:30-32. It wasn't his past causing the problem, but her ungodly response of bitterness, which the Bible warns us of in Hebrews 12:15.

She realized that she was nervous because her strong physical needs weren't being fulfilled. In addition, she was placing her husband in a terrible place of temptation by not meeting his physical needs, especially since this had been his weak area prior to salvation. I urged her to follow Ephesians 4:32 and forgive her husband completely and then to ask his forgiveness for the year and a half of punishment she had put him through.

She called a month later and said that her depression and nervousness had disappeared almost immediately, and her husband reported that the last month had been like one long honeymoon. Following God's principles helped

this woman to regain her own sense of stability
and brought happiness to her family life.

5 Praising God for Guidance

Over a period of years, hundreds of major and minor crises occur in the average family and cause instability: operations, prolonged illnesses, deaths, and tragic accidents. Broken bones, flu and minor home accidents are some of the lesser crises, but these too may be very upsetting if they occur in rapid succession. For example, if a man's wife ends up in the hospital with pneumonia, the washer breaks down, the transmission in the car gives out, and his 67-year-old widowed mother falls and breaks her hip—all within a short period of time— these individually minor crises may become a major problem.

Also these crisis periods increase proportionately with the number of children in the home, and the effects of each crisis may also increase considerably. Take for example the difference between one child coming down with the mumps and four children having them all at once.

In these crisis times, however, the family needs to look to God for His strength and power; for His grace is always sufficient. II Corinthians 12:9-10 reminds us of this principle. *"And he said unto me, My grace is sufficient for thee: for my strength is made perfect in weakness. Most gladly therefore will I rather glory in my infirmities, that the power of Christ may rest upon me. Therefore I take pleasure in infirmities, in reproaches, in necessities, in persecutions, in distresses for Christ's sake: for when I am weak, then am I strong."*

Ephesians 5:20 gives the key for overcoming any situation, *"Giving thanks always for all things unto God and the Father in the name of our Lord Jesus Christ."* I Thessalonians 5:18 emphasizes the same idea, *"In everything give thanks: for this is the will of God in Christ Jesus concerning you."* The ability to give thanks rests on the assurance found in Romans 8:28, *"And we know that all things work together for good to them that love God, to them who are the called according to his purpose."*

This principle was emphasized to me once as we were traveling to Florida. On our way we had a flat tire in the middle of a swamp in lower Georgia at 2:30 a.m. Initially the children had been asleep in the back seat, but in getting out the spare tire, I woke them up. Since the spare was half flat, I tried to pump some air into it. I was sweating, frustrated, and seemingly having no success at remedying the situation. As I was wrestling with the spare tire, one of my girls poked her head out of the window and asked, "Daddy, did you give thanks in everything? For this is the will of God in Christ Jesus concerning you." Of course I hadn't, so I bowed my head then and thanked God for the incident. A few minutes later she asked me why the Lord had let it happen. I told her that we may never know until we get to glory, but possibly the Lord wanted to protect us from a drunk driver down the road; God may have wanted to stop us long enough to get that driver off the road.

Giving thanks is a learned response, and getting into the habit of thanksgiving in small instances helps the Christian praise God in the larger, more crucial situations. For example, would a man *naturally* praise the Lord if one morning his wife came downstairs and said, "Honey, I think I'm pregnant," and he replied, "But you can't be, you're 43 years old"? Or would he praise the Lord on the morning he woke up and found that the creek behind his house had overflowed and swept half his yard down the block, especially since he had spent three months filling and landscaping it? We ought always to remember the admonition in Psalm 107:8. *"Oh that men would praise the Lord for his goodness, and for his wonderful works to the children of men!"*

Although losing a long-held job during a recession time strikes a critical blow to the family, the hardest single crisis is death, especially the death of a child. One of our friends lost two sons within the space of three years. Another friend was called and told that his four-year-old boy had accidentally shot and killed his two-year-old daughter. Still another lost his wife suddenly and was left with five children to rear alone. It is hard to give thanks in these situations for which there seems to be no reasonable explanation, but as Christians we must look to God for strength to do so.

Having a proper view of death and future glory can aid the Christian in times of tragedy. Philippians 1:21 gives a proper perspective, *"For to me to live is Christ, and to die is gain."* Christians must keep in mind that the best thing that can happen to them is to die and go to heaven. One day we, too, shall rejoice with our Saviour and with those loved ones who have gone before us. For these reasons we *"sorrow not, even as others which have no hope"* (I Thessalonians 4:13).

In any crisis situation, the Christian must remember three things: God's promises, His power, and His past performances.

God's Promises. God has given many promises of assurance in His Word. Every Christian would benefit from memorizing a backlog of these promises so that the Holy Spirit may easily bring them to mind when they're needed. God's promises will give divine perspective in every situation and peace in tragic times.

A friend of ours in Ohio lost his wife after she suffered from a pancreatic attack; then his son plunged off a Colorado mountainside to his death. His mother died; he lost all his money in a million-dollar apartment house foreclosure during a recession, and then lost his job as head of a large university department (a job he had held for 14 years). All of these crises happened within a two-year time span, but his faith remained strong throughout the trials because of his knowledge of God's promises.

God's Power. The same Lord who designed and made the universe, who multiplied the loaves and fishes and fed five thousand, who made man from the dust of the ground, and who willingly redeemed him can also bring all of His power to bear on man's problems. The Christian appropriates this power through faith, and the promises of God provide the rationale for this faith (Hebrews 4:2). God wants

Christians to pray, trusting Him to work out the problem to His honor and glory. He is all powerful and always willing to work in a life to bring about His perfect plan.

Finite man may not always conceive of how things are to be; but God knows the end from the beginning, and He knows exactly when and how to use His power for man's benefit. We saw evidence of this truth when a friend lost his job one morning. By the same evening he had received a phone call from 1000 miles away, offering him an unsolicited position with the opportunity of service he had long desired. God demonstrates His power by such perfect timing.

God's Past Performance. Familiarity destroys awareness. Many can remember the last time God worked a miracle—the time He answered a desperate prayer, the day He provided needed funds, the moment His hand protected a child from some catastrophe. But it is easy to forget God's daily blessings. Accustomed to benefiting from God's grace and protection, many Christians no longer seem awed by His power. They sometimes forget that the conception, growth and birth of a baby, the wonders of nature's cycles, and their very daily existence are all regular demonstrations of God's infinite power. Children should be introduced to these manifestations and made aware of the wonders of everyday life.

Children also need to be reminded of God's past personal blessings on the family. The Israelites, God's chosen people, had to be admonished constantly to remember God's past miracles. We often think back to the time when God took care of our

girl when she had a bone tumor in her arm. He paid
the doctor and hospital bills and healed the arm so it
grew normally. I remember also a $100 war bond
from a grandmother's estate that came within three
days of the deadline for a bill of that amount. The
war bond had been purchased for each grandchild 13
years earlier and was worth over $130 by the time
we needed it. All these incidents remind me of Isaiah
65:24, *"And it shall come to pass, that before they call, I will
answer; and while they are yet speaking I will hear."*

Children need to be taught early to have the
proper attitude toward God's working in their lives.
Preschoolers can learn I Thessalonians 5:18, and
Mother can help them to apply the Bible Action
Truth of giving thanks in everyday situations. One
mother helped her five-year-old daughter to utilize
this principle when the little girl's new birthday
dress was accidentally torn. Later, when the child's
pet cat died, she remembered the principle her
mother had taught her earlier, and after a little
crying she said, "Jesus said to give thanks, so I'd
better do it." Several months later when this same
little girl lost a contest; she prayed in family devotions, "Lord, I really don't feel it in my heart, but
thank you anyhow." She was learning.

Learning to thank and praise the Lord constantly
in daily situations (Psalm 107:8) makes every day a
bit of heaven and gets the Christian ready for
heaven, where he will be praising the Lord for His
creation (Revelation 4:10, 11) and for His redemption (Revelation 5:9, 10). The Christian should, with
David, make a vow to praise the Lord seven times a
day (Psalm 119:164).

Disappointments become God's appointments

when Christians look for God's hand in their daily lives. Maybe there is a doctor, nurse, or patient God wants to reach through a Christian's unexpected hospital experience. A new business opportunity or contact may be the outcome of a Christian's completely frustrated plans. A unique ministry may result from a tragedy or heartache. One large deaf ministry came about as a result of a deaf girl being born into the family of the founder of the organization. Only when a Christian yields to the Lord can God direct him in all of his daily affairs.

When disappointments come, I am often reminded of the song, "Back of the Clouds the Sun is Always Shining." Taking off in a jet on a black, stormy day is always a thrilling experience; within minutes there is a burst of sunlight—below, the clouds look black, but from the top they look as white as snow. God's love is much like the sun, sometimes obscured by life's problems, but the Christian may be assured that it is always there. A positive faith attitude results from "giving thanks for all things" and letting God run the show.

6 The Submission Attitude

Wifely submission is not a popular concept in modern America. The women's liberation movement considers the idea offensive, old-fashioned, and unjust. But every Christian wife is told in Scripture to submit to her husband just as she submits to Christ.

What does it mean to be submissive? Does it mean that a wife must give up all initiative, all creativity? On the contrary, Proverbs 31 makes it clear that a woman can be creative and have initiative even within the framework of her submissive role.

The secret of total submission is a servant's attitude. The servant's attitude is two-fold, and the story of Mary and Martha offers us a choice illustration. In Luke 10:38-42 Martha is concerned about the Lord's comforts, and Mary is concerned about adoration and nearness to Him. A wife who desires a proper servant's attitude should notice that both of these types of service are necessary but that Jesus Christ commended Mary for choosing the better role.

Many wives are wonderful servants to their families and husbands in providing meals, clothes, and a clean environment, but they fail to understand other needs for the personal attentions of a devoted wife. An adoring attitude is a crucial part of real love-submission. A woman trying to win a husband shows this attitude continuously before marriage, and the man responds with a tender protective love for her. After marriage, however, the woman often becomes burdened with the cares of the household and neglects the most important responsibility of caring for her husband's psychological need for love and companionship. Instead of submitting to their husbands, many women use the following means to control them.

Scheduling. The domineering woman uses well-ordered household schedules to bring her husband under the same authority that the children are under. She uses such comments as "If you want supper, you must be here at exactly 6:00" or "If you have any regard for your family, you will run these errands immediately." Togetherness is vital to an effectively-run household, and the husband and wife should *cooperate* in accomplishing goals.

Spending. A wife may also use charge cards and time payments to keep her husband continually off balance financially and make it necessary for him to work harder to pay the bills. When he objects, she may make him feel guilty by comparing her situation to a friend. It is interesting to note that more problems are caused by finances than by any other circumstance in marriage.

Sex. Some women also use sex as a weapon in the daily relationship. To gain control, this type of woman is loving, eager, and receptive; but if she cannot dominate the situation, she becomes cold and negative. Generally, a woman who is stubborn and rebellious toward men overall (and her husband in particular) finds no real pleasure in the physical relationship. She cannot stand the idea of complete submission and abandonment to her husband that provides the necessary part of supreme enjoyment.

Sickness. Convenient backaches, headaches, or general aches and pains can be a good excuse for adapting the husband's careful planning to fit the wife's desires. "Trouble with nerves" is usually nothing more than a selfish method of making family activities revolve around the wife.

Sobbing. A woman may use tears to get her way in important matters. Men feel helpless and somewhat brutish when confronted by tears. Their instincts tell them that men are supposed to make women happy; therefore, they must give in to the wife's wishes. A woman soon learns when the tears will be most effective in accomplishing her purposes.

Spirituality. Unfortunately, some women are far ahead of their husbands spiritually, and some use this "spiritual superiority" to gain control of the family. "The Lord led me to do this" or "the Lord revealed that to me in His Word" brings the husband into submission—for what husband dares argue against the Lord's will? This subtle technique becomes more effective, but at the same time undermines the basis of marriage, when the wife constantly compares her three hours a day of Bible study to her husband's ten-minute devotional time.

Silence. Refusing to speak, or doing so grudgingly, can be a powerful tool to get one's own way. "I won't talk until you do what I want" is the unspoken implication.

Suicide or Divorce Threats. A few women have gone to the extreme of suggesting divorce or threatening suicide to gain control of a crucial situation. These women desperately need a strong, consistent husband who will take full control of the situation and provide for them the security they lack.

A woman who usurps the authority properly belonging to her husband is in danger of causing physical and psychological harm to the children in the family. Researchers have found that delinquent children usually come from homes in which the mother dominated and the father lacked authority. This statistic is especially true of delinquent boys. In certain segments of our population where delinquency runs high, approximately 25 percent of the homes lack male leadership or are run by a mother who is very domineering because she has a better job than her husband. One of the key factors in the background of homosexuals (especially males) is a strong, domineering, overly possessive mother and a weak, ineffectual father.

Christian viewpoints on a woman's submission vary greatly. A widespread idea is that since Ephesians 5:24 states that a woman must be submissive in everything, it means just that. Even if a woman is asked by her husband to commit adultery or to act immorally in another situation, she is obliged to do as he says. Those who hold this idea believe that God will hold the man responsible for the wife's actions (Genesis 12:11-20, Numbers 30:6-16). Proponents of this view also hold that if a woman is submissive in all areas of her life and is much in prayer regarding the immoral command, God will change the heart of the husband who made the sinful request (Proverbs 21:1) and spare her from violating God's law.

A differing viewpoint has been offered by a well-known Christian worker's wife who says that Ephesians 5:24 is conditioned by the phrase in Ephesians 5:22 which says "unto the Lord." A wife does not have to submit to her husband if he gives her a command that in any way violates her conscience. This could include the way she dresses, the discipline of the children, and other unspecified moral situations.

This passage in Ephesians 5 is the key to submission. Verses 22-24 indicate that wives are to submit themselves to their own husbands "as unto the Lord." The husband is the head of the wife even as Christ is head of the church. The protective nature of the husband is compared to that of Jesus Christ, who is the Saviour of the body. Verse 24 says that the wife is to submit to her husband in everything, just as the church is submissive to Christ. The question which needs to be answered is "Whose authority is the wife to submit to when God's commands and the husband's commands conflict?" The principle of Matthew 22:21 applies in all our authority relationships. We are to render to Caesar what is Caesar's and to God what is God's: we must always submit to the higher authority. If a mother told her child one thing and the father told him the opposite, the child would be obligated to submit to his father, who is the higher authority. If a wife were asked by her husband to do something that God had forbidden in His Word, she would have to submit to God for He is the highest authority. There are, however, certain things a husband may command his wife to do that are not in violation of Scripture. In these cases the wife is to obey him.

The phrase "unto the Lord" in verse 22 also indicates the wife's voluntary servant's attitude toward her husband. She is to have the same attitude toward him as Christians are to have toward God. This same principle applies to a woman who has been saved since marriage but whose husband is not right with the Lord. I Peter 3:1-6 tells her how she can win him, not by nagging or preaching at him, but by exhibiting the inner beauty of a meek and quiet spirit (verse 4). Verse 3 indicates that while outward beauty may fade, inner beauty, a meek and quiet spirit, is incorruptible. Verse 6 tells us that Sarah obeyed Abraham "calling him Lord." Because of her sweet, submissive attitude, she was blessed by God with a loving, adoring husband and a long-desired son.

Titus 2:4-5 says that the older women are to *"teach the young women to be sober, to love their husbands, to love their children, to be discreet, chaste, keepers at home, good, obedient to their husbands, that the word of God be not blasphemed."* Obedience and submission are to be given with a sincere attitude of love. This attitude does not enslave, but gives the wife security in the bond of love.

One rebellious young Christian wife, whose husband was unsaved, frequently complained of nervousness and depression. However, one day she came from a conference on the family having made up her mind to apply the principle of submission. She announced to her husband that she had gotten right with the Lord and apologized for being an improper wife. She began consciously to encourage him and let him make the decisions. She didn't argue but was physically responsive and eager. Her husband at first tested her by being somewhat unreasonable and overbearing, but after two months, when he saw that the change was permanent, he began going to church with her. He was saved, and they both are now active workers in the church. Not only was her marriage improved beyond her most idealistic dreams, but her depression and nervousness disappeared also. Perseverance is requisite for such situations.

The average woman does not instinctively seek the submissive position, but learning to give the husband the lead will give her a tremendous psychological security and eliminate many frustrations from her life. If, however, there are children, she should remember that she is in authority over them (for their good) and they are the bottom of the hierarchy of care and authority.

Serving the husband as unto the Lord will promote family unity as well as insure God's approval on the home. The Scripture instructs about God's way and warns against the devil's way. The following checklist will help the wife to see herself in the light of these two choices:

Satan's Way
1. With a railing and contentious spirit (I Peter 3:9; Proverbs 19:13b)
2. By withdrawing from his affections and being

cold (I Corinthians 7:3-5)

3. With an unresponsive and unsympathetic ear (Proverbs 12:25)

4. With resentment of his service for the Lord (II Samuel 6:20-23)

5. With unanswered prayers because of wrong attitudes (I Peter 3:7)

6. With an uncaring attitude for her appearance (I Corinthians 10:31)

7. With jealousy for other women's positions or abilities (James 3:14)

8. With a destructive attitude (Proverbs 14:1b)

9. With a discontented and selfish spirit (I Timothy 6:6-8)

10. As a rottenness to his bones (Proverbs 12:4b)

God's Way

1. With a meek and quiet spirit (I Peter 3:4)

2. With a desire to please her husband (Genesis 3:16; I Corinthians 7:34)

3. With consolation and support (loyalty) (Genesis 24:67; Proverbs 31:11)

4. With a willingness to be of help and to help the children understand what Dad is doing (Genesis 2:18)

5. With reverence and obedience (Ephesians 5:33; I Peter 3:5, 6)

6. With strength of body—weight control, exercise, and rest (Proverbs 31:17)

7. With strength of mind (Philippians 2:5; I Peter 1:13; II Timothy 1:7)

8. With a desire to keep the home a place where he may come for comfort and rest (Titus 2:5; Proverbs 31:27; Proverbs 14:1)

9. With a hospitable attitude toward his friends and others in need (Proverbs 31:20; Romans 3:10; Romans 12:13)

10. As a crown to him (Proverbs 12:4a)

7 Love and Leadership

A woman, because of her basic nature, reacts best to a husband who is a strong leader-lover. She wants to be led and tends to respond and follow. She also needs tenderness and affection, for this fulfills her need for security as discussed in chapter three.

Some men have a problem achieving a balance between the two roles of love and leadership. A man may either be too aggressive, treating his wife like a slave or he may be too passive, doing anything to placate his wife. He may also just be indifferent to her.

There is a way to achieve this needed balance, and God gives us the formula in Ephesians 5:25-30. Verse 25 commands, *"Husbands, love your wives, even as Christ also loved the church, and gave himself for it."* Verse 23 points out the scriptural analogy of the man representing Christ and the woman the church or body of believers. Consequently, in verse 25a man is to have the same dynamic leadership that Christ gives to His church while at the same time possessing a love that would prompt sacrifice—even the sacrifice of death.

A man's leadership involves a full awareness of his position as the head of the family. He's not equal with the wife, but the leader. When two people are riding a horse, one person must be up front holding the reins; the other must be seated behind him.

The husband's leadership in the home also demands the same responsible actions as in any other leadership endeavor. He must plan, make decisions, organize, delegate authority, and supervise activity. The applications of these leadership functions will, of course, vary, but the essentials remain the same.

Planning. Many times a husband is a mere spectator in his marriage; he watches and reacts to what happens, but he doesn't control what is happening. He becomes a victim of circumstances; consequently, his family life becomes frustrating and meaningless. It is important that a husband sit down with his wife to plan the budget, social activities, projects, home furnishings, purchases, spiritual activities, and holiday celebrations. A couple must do these things together—with the husband taking the lead role.

This planning stage need not be drudgery. Half of the fun of doing things is in planning and anticipating the event. A wedding anniversary should be an exciting, special time. For example, a couple could plan a trip to the regional outdoor historical play and visit a unique mountainside motel. They may be the types who would enjoy an exotic meal in a famous restaurant, a weekend at the ocean, or a drive along a beautiful parkway. All of these are ideas that can make a "special event" even more enjoyable, but these kinds of things need creative planning, and it is the husband's responsibility to make certain that things are well in order.

Such planning, however, does not exclude the possibility of surprises or spontaneous activities like taking a ride on the shopping center ferris wheel or stopping at a quaint antique shop on the way home from visiting the in-laws. Planning must also be flexible enough to make room for emergencies or even for mood changes. Many times we have decided on the spur of the moment to have a quiet evening at home rather than to attend some preplanned activity. Sometimes resting or diverting attention is necessary to prevent problems that might be caused by the daily pressures of busy activities. Good planning can alleviate a lot of unnecessary burden, and a planning calendar is a terrific idea to help in this matter.

Deciding. Decision comes before purposeful action. After obtaining sufficient facts from various sources and consulting his wife, the husband must make the final, big decision. Once he makes a decision, he should take action; the time for questioning should come *before*, not after, the decision. As he makes and implements wise decisions, he builds confidence that makes future decisions easier to make. Men make mistakes, but the husband must be flexible enough to reverse or adjust a bad decision—God can help him learn through his mistakes (Proverbs 21:1). Acknowledging God by praying for His leadership will assure the husband of the Holy Spirit's leadership in his daily decision-making responsibilities.

Organizing. Family leaders must organize rather

than agonize. How is a husband going to carry out his plan? What materials does he need? What people need to be contacted? Can this activity dovetail with another plan and thus save some time and energy?

We used to organize our trips to church on Wednesday nights, and by doing so we saved ourselves a great deal of effort. On the way we would stop at the shopping center to get any needed items; we would then go to the Sunday school teacher's meeting, then prayer meeting, and finally attend some meeting after church or counsel with a church member. We could also usually get one Sunday school visit in before 9:30 and then wind up the evening at the grocery store for the week's groceries. The church helped in this organization by scheduling many meetings on Wednesday evenings, and our regular supermarket conveniently stayed open until 11 p.m. This type of planning helps to get shopping done in one trip rather than two or three trips daily or weekly.

Delegating. A father needs to delegate the details of any operation. A simple picnic in the park demands much cooperation to make the experience pleasurable. While Mother takes care of the menu planning and Dad takes care of the outdoor cooking, the children can assist in setting things up and cleaning up after everything is over. Whatever the activity, each family member should have a specific job so things can run smoothly. Household chores should also be delegated; far too many times Mother is left with all the clean-up. This help is especially important for big events such as a family reunion or a holiday celebration. Each child's making his own bed, carrying his own dishes to the sink, and putting his belongings in their proper place will aid in running an efficient household.

Supervising. A good leader not only organizes, but also supervises. He's responsible and handles or solves problems rather than placing the blame. A real leader is a buffer or shock absorber for the big problems of life. Dumping the big problems on his wife or family communicates weakness and causes the wife and children to feel insecure. He also checks up to make sure that details are being carried out as they have been delegated; he must inspect what he expects. Making out a checklist for certain activities is helpful, especially for camping trips and outings.

The children learn leadership responsibility from the father's example. Therefore, it is important not only that the father plan, delegate, decide, organize, and supervise, but also that he pitch in and carry his share of the load.

Joshua 24:14, 15 gives us a view of one of the great leaders of the Israelites, *"As for me and my house, we will serve the Lord."* Positive leadership qualities are also indicated in I Timothy 3:4, where the elders of the church are described as leaders in their homes, *"He ruleth well his own house, having his children in subjection with all gravity."* Even the deacons in verse 12 are to be *"ruling their children and their own houses well."*

In the verses we have pointed out, the word *rule* actually means "manage." It is important to note that leadership has two facets: the management of things and the management of people. The leader of the family needs to balance the two. Many fathers excel in the management of things (the car, yard, workshop, budget, etc.), but they tend to neglect the management of the people in their own household.

A real leader, however, does not display a dictator attitude. People who are thrust into leadership roles without any prior knowledge of what a leader is to do will often quickly assume the role of the dictator. The Christian wife needs a leader who is willing to work continuously on his leadership role. A wife will willingly follow her husband if he will lead, but the wife may rebel against a man who is a dictator. If a husband will love his wife as Christ loves the church, he will gently lead, not bulldoze, her.

Leadership, as mentioned earlier, must be balanced with love, as Christ loves the church. To be properly balanced, a husband must follow the Lord's example. First, he must have a willingness to sacrifice—even unto death, as Christ did for us on the cross (Ephesians 5:25). When a man marries, he must be prepared to sacrifice his money, time, emotions, and physical strength for his wife and later also for his children.

For example, John was a well-adjusted, self-sufficient Christian with $8,000 saved for investment purposes. His $12,000 per year job enabled him to live comfortably with plenty of time for tennis, swimming, hunting, fishing, reading, and travel. He was also active in a local church, teaching Sunday school and heading up a Pro-Teen club. He married a lovely Christian girl and seemed to be heading for success.

Seven years later he was in my office bemoaning his fate. He had four children, a $35,000 mortgage, and only $300 savings in the bank. He complained that his $20,000 per year salary was not leaving anything for extras like a vacation, a deer hunting license, or materials for his photography hobby. He said, "I don't have the time, energy, or money to have fun anymore. It seems that I'm always being called on to sacrifice my desires for my wife and kids and getting nothing in return—not even a love life because my wife is so fatigued."

I pointed out that this was what mature love was all about. Instead of being concerned with his own selfish interests, John needed to start doing what was necessary to serve and meet the needs of his loved ones. He could find his joy in their happiness and fulfillment.

I outlined a few things he could do in working with the children such as playing games with them, teaching his four- and five-year-old boys to swim and fish, and taking his whole family on a camping trip. Regarding his wife, they decided to have a girl come in after school every afternoon to care for the children and babysit one evening a week. The husband sold and installed smoke alarms one evening a week to supply the extra $25 per week it cost him for the added help. He also started planning and working on happy times, especially on their evenings out. He and his wife took several weekend vacations alone including a couples' retreat at a Christian camp. He began to see that the more sacrifice he made, the more fruits he realized for his love. He later said, "I guess this is the fun of living—giving to others."

Verse 26 of Ephesians 5 gives the second way that Christ loves the church, *"The washing of water by the word."* Christ loves us in providing His Word whereby He constantly *communicates* with us. His

Word has a cleansing effect on us as we confess our needs to Him in prayer; this love welds us to our Saviour. The husband must talk to his wife daily and listen to her problems and needs; even though they may seem mundane and trite compared to his business day, they are not.

Several years ago we made an interesting survey of a number of Christian women. We asked them, "What does your husband do that makes you feel loved?" We compiled the answers in order of importance and frequency. The top seven became a guide to husbands on how to love their wives. The first on this list of seven deals with communication.

A sympathetic awareness and understanding of the wife's simple everyday problems best communicates love to a wife. The typical housewife and mother of preschoolers gets into a humdrum role of diapers, dishes, and drudgery. After answering a thousand "why" questions and talking to two- and three-year-olds all day, she begins to wonder if she will ever again carry on an adult conversation.

Many problems arise that she would like to discuss with a sympathetic listener—someone who will give her his undivided attention, nodding and responding to her conversation. Discussion will help keep the vital unity in a marriage.

A well-to-do businessman confided that his marriage seemed to be losing its vitality until he realized his indifference in responding to his wife's problems. He confessed that the stock market and sports page of the newspaper were convenient escapes from her seemingly endless chatter. A wonderful change came about in their relationship when he started folding his newspaper, putting it aside, and attentively listening each time she began talking to him.

Thoughtfulness in little things goes a long way. The loving husband calls if he will be late to supper, and he may occasionally bring home a small gift such as a candy bar or a flower. He might also bathe and put the children to bed after a big trip.

It's not the big things that really count, but the small daily remembrances that make the difference. A wife on a special diet from hypoglycemia does not need a five-pound box of candy for Valentine's day, but a small candy bar and a love poem will show that her husband remembered her. Likewise, when she goes to do the dishes, a love note pinned to the kitchen curtains will remind her of her husband's appreciation for all she does daily.

Verbal assurance is also vital. Women generally need three compliments a day. Many women feel inadequate and inferior and need constant reassurance that they are superior mothers, lovers, housekeepers, cooks, and creative people. Each needs to know that she is lovely in her husband's eyes. Complimenting a wife on her physical appearance in front of friends and children will do wonders for her self-esteem.

Wives want their husbands to notice the things they do. The special housecleaning, the new centerpiece, the special dinner—all deserve notice. Verse 27 of Ephesians 5 says that Christ is trying to help the church become spotless, without blemish, and a husband's assurance and encouragement will have this same cleansing effect on his wife. Criticism, sarcasm, and belittling serve only to damage the woman's self-concept and affect how she reacts to her husband. A husband's verbal reaction becomes the mirror through which the wife sees herself.

Physical attention also assures the wife of her husband's love. Women are touch-oriented; even in love-making most women require a lot of gentle stimulation for maximum response. At tender or crisis moments a squeeze of the hand or a protecting arm around her will give her a tremendous sense of security. Women need a lot of affection and cuddling to satisfy their security need.

A positive attitude helps too. The little situations as well as the big events need a positive, dynamic solution. A negative approach will increase insecure feelings and cause a wife to mistrust her husband's ability to handle a situation. In everyday occurrences the husband needs to stay off the defensive and concentrate on positively solving the problems which arise. Instead of waiting for his wife to nag him to carry out the garbage, a husband could make it part of his daily routine and tell his wife he loves her as he takes it out on his way to work.

Feeling needed is the sixth most valuable way to show a wife she is loved. Every woman wants to feel needed. She wants to be part of her husband's life and to feel fulfilled in her contributions to the family unity. A husband can show her he needs her by daily recognizing her contributions and letting her know how much he appreciates the things she does for him and the children.

"I feel loved when my husband is right with the Lord," was another reply of several women, indicating the spiritual nature of love. The husband's taking the lead in Bible reading, praying, and church participation assures the wife of God's hand on the marriage.

To love his wife properly—to balance his duties as leader and protector—a husband must understand his wife's individual needs as well as the general needs of every woman. Then he must use his imagination to try to fulfill these needs and desires.

Ephesians 5:28, 29 states, *"So ought men to love their wives as their own bodies. He that loveth his wife loveth himself. For no man ever yet hated his own flesh; but nourisheth and cherisheth it, even as the Lord the church."* A man nourishes his wife by providing for her physical needs. The house, food, and luxuries are provided for through his paycheck, and the hard work that goes into earning the check is the husband's way of saying, "I love you."

The Scripture is clear concerning God's attitude toward an indolent husband. I Timothy 5:8 says, *"But if any provide not for his own, and specially for those of his own house, he hath denied the faith, and is worse than an infidel."* A caring man always figures out how to earn needed additional funds through an extra sales or repair job or possibly by using his gardening talents or his refinishing and upholstering abilities. He might also save money by doing his own car and home repairs. Since work is man's forte, the wife recognizes his loving concern in meeting the family's physical needs when the husband fulfills his responsibilities financially.

Cherishing a wife is a learned art and fathers ought to teach their sons to do so early in life. The godly husband treats his wife gently and patiently and has a protecting respect for her weakness.

I Peter 3:7 says, *"Likewise, ye husbands, dwell with them according to knowledge, giving honour unto the wife, as unto the weaker vessel, and as being heirs together of the grace of life; that your prayers be not hindered."* A good husband will realize that his wife is weaker physically and psychologically and will treat her accordingly; he will thus guard against making her nervous, neurotic, or constantly irritated.

The general guide for the proper attitude toward the wife is given in Ephesians 5:28 when it states, *"So ought men to love their wives as their own bodies. He that loveth his wife loveth himself."* Men are particularly protective of their bodies and tend to pamper or favor an injured part. If a husband takes this principle into consideration, he will be especially protective and sympathetic when his wife is ill. Of course, under no circumstance should a husband physically abuse his wife; instead he should be certain that his sons are trained to protect rather than strike or fight with girls. A boy who sees his father come to the aid of a woman in distress on the highway soon learns these basic ideas on how to treat women.

Cherishing a wife involves reacting properly to her personal needs and desires. Taking the kids to the park when his wife is especially tired or taking them on a camping trip or some other weekend excursion while she visits her mother is exemplary of a good, loving husband. Being extra considerate about her likes and desires makes for harmony in the home. For example, my wife never really cared about sitting in a boat fishing at 5 a.m., but she was glad to cook the fish I had caught (once they had been completely cleaned). So I enjoyed fishing, but I also cleaned the fish before I gave them to her to cook. Understanding is the key to cherishing a woman.

Bitterness is an attitude that can destroy any marriage, and husbands are especially warned against this in Colossians 3:19, *"Husbands, love your wives and be not bitter against them."* A bitter attitude toward the wife creates a negative mental attitude. For example, a husband starts comparing his wife to other younger or more desirable women. He begins to bicker with her and constantly belittles her unfairly; eventually, he becomes indifferent, and verbal and physical communication breaks down. Then fantasy and lust become a problem. All warm emotional feelings die, and impotency usually follows. Bitterness is usually the cause of male impotency (failure to perform in the physical relationship), though it may result from poor health, extreme fatigue, diabetes, tranquilizers, or drugs (especially those used for high blood pressure).

One 31-year-old man who had been married eight years and had three children came to see me about the problem of lusting after other women. The real problem was that for the last year and a half he could not perform with his wife most of the time. After finding out that there was no physical reason for his problem, I inquired about bitterness. He admitted that he had become bitter against his wife after she had pressured him to buy a home beyond their means. This financial overextension had given her an excuse to go back to work, a situation he opposed. When she then became too tired for love and rejected him numerous times, he had become bitter.

The solution was recognizing the cause and

allowing God to rid him of the root of bitterness. After talking over their problem and readjusting their finances, she was able to cut down her working time. Her conviction of the importance of meeting his needs solved the problem.

Bitterness, if not eliminated, can push a man into a "devil set-up" with a strange woman. Interestingly, the Bible doesn't warn women about men, but in Proverbs men are admonished to stay away from "strange women" (Proverbs 5, 6, 7 and the last part of chapter 9). Women must realize that if their husbands are emotionally and physically hungry, they may be attracted to this type of woman.

Husbands and wives must continuously work at keeping the unity in their marriage. When a husband starts taking creative leadership in love, his wife responds, and the whole family reaps the benefits of happiness.

8 One-Flesh Unity

The ultimate unity in marriage is the one-flesh principle given in Ephesians 5:31-33, *"For this cause shall a man leave his father and mother, and shall be joined unto his wife, and they two shall be one flesh. This is a great mystery: but I speak concerning Christ and the church. Nevertheless let every one of you in particular so love his wife even as himself; and the wife see that she reverence her husband."* In verse 31, we see the words, *"joined unto his wife."* The word *joined* means "glued together" and indicates a unity which God does not want divided. The next phrase, *"and they two shall be one flesh,"* refers to the physical relationship first mentioned in Genesis 2:24.

Marriage culminates in physical oneness; it is the unique identification of two complementary, but opposite individuals, male and female. This unity, according to God's sovereign plan, may result in having children.

There is a great contrast between Scripture's one-flesh relationship and "sex" as the world perceives it. The word *sex* from the world's viewpoint connotes filth, corruption, and pornography. The

current program of sex education excludes any kind
of morality. Therefore, I think Christians should
prefer the Bible term, "one-flesh," when speaking of
the physical relationship. Looking at the Scripture
and considering the various principles concerning
this unity, the Christian should notice that the Bible
makes an important distinction between this beautiful union and the world's tainted interpretation of
the one-flesh principle.

One purpose of the one-flesh relationship is to
illustrate the unity between Christ and His Church.
This truth is brought out in the 32nd verse of Ephesians 5. The great mystery is that Christ is in us,
Colossians 1:27, *"Christ in you, the hope of glory,"* and
that we are in Christ; II Corinthians 5:17, *"Therefore
if any man be in Christ, he is a new creature."* Therefore,
the beauty of the marriage union is actually in its
illustration of the union of Christ to His bride, the
church. Verse 33 draws the analogy clearly by
bringing the illustration back to the husband-wife
relationship.

Reproduction is a second reason for the one-
flesh relationship (Genesis 1:28). The Christian
should be fruitful, having children and training
them to glorify the Lord. A third reason for this
union is to avoid fornication (I Corinthians 7:2), and
a fourth is for companionship (Genesis 2:18). The
one-flesh relationship is the closest, most pleasurable communion between a man and woman. In
marriage it can be experienced with all the legal,
moral, and spiritual blessings—in marriage this
union should produce no guilt feelings whatever.

The first principle to remember about the one-
flesh relationship is that **God has ordained this**

relationship and placed His stamp of approval upon it. In Hebrews 13:4, we read, *"Marriage is honourable in all, and the bed undefiled."* Consequently, this verse assures the married couple that they should be able to pray together and thank God for each other after this time of union.

Many men complain that the more spiritual their wives seem to be, the more involved in church-related activities, the less they are interested in the one-flesh union. These wives are missing the main purpose of this relationship, that of welding the husband and wife together as co-laborers in their God-given ministry. If there is unity in this husband-wife relationship, the two will be able, to-gether, to reach out effectively to others. Hebrews 13:4, however, also gives us a warning. Though God has ordained the one-flesh relationship in the con-text of marriage, He hates (and will ultimately judge) sexual relationships outside of marriage. Verse 4 specifically states, *"but whoremongers and adulterers God will judge."*

Some may think of the marital relationship as sinful. This misconception is due to these Chris-tians' distorted ideas about their own bodies. Born-again believers need to be reminded that their bodies are the temple of the Holy Spirit. When God created man, He declared His creation good. Our bodies become the temple of the Holy Ghost when we are saved; they are good and wonderful in God's eyes.

The reason for Scripture's command to cover the body and the warning against the children's looking upon their parents' nakedness is to avoid sinful lust which results from seeing a naked body. Even in the

home, the prohibition of bodily display helps to prevent incest and other forms of corruption. Men are
sight-oriented, and women should be careful to
dress discreetly so that they do not tempt men.
However, there should be no shame connected to
nakedness between the husband and his wife.

The second principle given in Proverbs 5:15-19
**indicates the proper viewpoint concerning the one-
flesh relationship.** *"Drink waters out of thine own cistern,
and running waters out of thine own well. Let thy fountains be
dispersed abroad, and rivers of waters in the streets. Let them be
only thine own, and not strangers' with thee. Let thy fountain
be blessed: and rejoice with the wife of thy youth. Let her be as
the loving hind and pleasant roe; let her breasts satisfy thee at
all times; and be thou ravished always with her love."* Although this section uses agricultural terms, the
meaning is clear. Verse 15, *"Drink waters out of thine
own cistern, and running waters out of thine own well,"* refers to the one-flesh relationship—every man
having his own wife and every woman having her
own husband. Verses 16 and 17 then refer to having
children, *"Let thy fountains be dispersed abroad, and rivers of
waters in the streets. Let them be only thine own and not strangers' with thee."* God is against communal living. He
has ordained that a married couple be the mother
and the father of children that He blesses them
with, making a godly family. The Bible indicates in
Psalm 127:3-5 that children are a heritage of the
Lord. They are like arrows in the hand of a mighty
man. Psalm 128:3 states, *"Thy wife shall be as a fruitful
vine by the sides of thine house: thy children like olive plants
round about thy table."* Proverbs 5:17 also attests that
children are the natural parents' responsibility. God
has established the family—one mother and father

taking care of their own children.

Proverbs 5:18 encourages the husband and wife to rejoice in the one-flesh relationship. *"Let thy fountain be blessed, and rejoice with the wife of thy youth."* The Scriptures also suggest that the wife be eager and receptive toward her husband. For verse 19 states, *"Let her be as a loving hind and a pleasant roe."* Joseph Dillow in his commentary on the Song of Solomon, *Solomon on Sex,* gives a number of helpful suggestions.

If Christians are to preserve the sweet unity of this relationship in their marriage, they must heed a third principle, given in I Corinthians 7:1-5 which says that **the husband or wife should never refuse his or her spouse the joy of the one-flesh relationship.** More questions, conflicts, and disagreements arise over this one point in the one-flesh relationship than over any other facet. The problems are answered simply in Scripture. The principle is that the husband and wife should unselfishly, self-sacrificially, and lovingly meet the other partner's physical need regardless of how frequently that desire needs to be met.

I Corinthians 7:1 deals with another caution. The verse states, *"Now concerning the things whereof ye wrote unto me: It is good for a man not to touch a woman."* The phrase, *"not to touch,"* means not to kindle a sexual desire in her. The man should not kindle a sexual desire in a woman, nor should a woman kindle such a desire in a man, unless they are husband and wife. Verse 2 tells us why: *"Nevertheless, to avoid fornication, let every man have his own wife, and let every woman have her own husband."* The one-flesh relationship in marriage is given to Christians to avoid fornication.

A second step in avoiding fornication is found in verse 3 of I Corinthians 7, which states, *"Let the husband render unto the wife due benevolence: and likewise also the wife unto the husband."* A husband is expected to give her the physical love that is due her, and the wife is to do the same for her husband. Verse 4 further states that *"The wife hath not power of her own body, but the husband: and likewise also the husband hath not power of his own body, but the wife."* The one exception to this principle is given in verse 5, *"Defraud ye not one another, except it be with consent for a time, that ye may give yourselves to fasting and prayer; and come together again, that Satan tempt you not for your incontinency."* A married couple may take a short time—a day or two—for prayer and fasting, but there must be mutual agreement on the matter. Following this agreed time of prayer and fasting, they are to come together again that they may avoid temptation.

A woman may complain that her husband thinks only about the physical aspect of marriage. She may say that he doesn't really love her as a person. Those who have this complaint should realize several things. First of all, a husband says "I love you" through physical love-making. Secondly, Psalm 19:5 seems to imply that a spiritual, emotional, and physical strength can be derived from this unity of love: *"As a bridegroom coming out of his chamber and rejoiceth as a strong man to run a race."* Thirdly, any bodily need becomes predominant in our thinking if the need goes unsatisfied. A person in the desert has a strong dominant desire for water, but this need disappears when he stands by a water cooler, able to drink as much as he wants. One can reasonably conclude that a man desperately hungry for physical love is probably not having his need met. The wife must both know and meet her husband's needs— especially if his job makes it necessary for him to travel extensively. The truck driver's wife or the salesman's wife needs to be sure that her husband's needs are met before he leaves and that she meets them when he returns. He will then be far less likely to be tempted by Satan when he is away.

A husband, too, must be aware of his wife's normal physical needs. He should reserve a good time for love. Many think that bedtime is the only appropriate time for physical love, but this is often the time when women are most fatigued. The morning or noontime, while the kids are at school, and even early evening, once the children are in bed, are all appropriate times. Taking the phone off the hook will assure that these times of rest and love are not disturbed.

Both men and women want affection and adoration through physical love. The words spoken, the kisses, and fondling, and the cherishing afterwards are all part of the real unity of the one-flesh relationship. Partners of those from unhappy home backgrounds should be ready to give a double dose of love and affection to make up for the love missed during childhood. Eager availability is the chief technique in a loving wife's repertoire for keeping her husband happy and satisfied.

A fourth general principle is that **the wife should be able to experience extreme enjoyment during the one-flesh relationship.** If she cannot enjoy the relationship, she will be reluctant to participate and adequately meet her husband's needs. Though the

Bible does not specifically refer to this principle, allusions to pleasure and enjoyment on the part of the wife are noted in the Song of Solomon. In this Song the wife seems to be an eager, sensual participant, who thoroughly enjoys this relationship with her husband.

In the last few years several extensive studies have been done on women's reactions and responses in this area of the physical relationship. The *Redbook* survey of 100,000 women and the *Psychology Today* survey of 25,000 women both revealed a number of interesting points concerning the wife's responses. It was noted that approximately 40 percent of the women enjoy the physical relationship half the time or less. Twenty percent never enjoy it, and only 45 percent reach this extreme enjoyment most of the time. Sixteen percent of those do so several times on most occasions. These statistics are fairly close to those gathered in earlier studies.

In his 1973 study of 300 women, Seymour Fisher determined many reasons for frigidity or lack of response. Marie Robinson also discusses several causes and gives steps for overcoming frigidity in her book *The Power of Sexual Surrender*. Some of the causes noted by these and other researchers are as follows:

A poor self-concept. A husband can do much to alleviate his wife's problem in this area by building her up and making her feel like a worthwhile person.

A lack of a submissive spirit. Frigid women tend to rebel against men in general and their husbands in particular. A woman's extreme enjoyment in the one-flesh relationship hinges on her giving herself over to her husband completely.

Lack of concentration on their bodily feelings. This is one complaint many men have about their wives. They note that the wife doesn't put her mind on matters at hand but is easily distracted by a crying baby or other extraneous interruptions. Tim LaHaye's book, *The Act of Marriage*, gives some very helpful information.

Insecure feelings or hidden fears of loss and separation. Again, the husband can do a great deal in alleviating his wife's insecure feelings by assuring her of his love. Day-by-day assurances such as hugging her, holding her in his arms, and assuring her of his protection can solve this problem.

Guilt feelings, especially about moral matters. This cause is the reason for the admonition in I Corinthians 6:18, *"Flee fornication,"* which is a broad term referring to all types of sexual sins. Also, *"Every sin that a man doeth is without the body; but he that committeth fornication sinneth against his own body."* This verse seems to point out that fornication is prone to have more damaging physical and psychological effects than any other type of sin.

Anyone suffering from guilt feelings needs to take heed to the three-point formula for getting rid of sin boils (moral sins) in the life. *"For the kingdom of God is not meat and drink; but righteousness, and peace, and joy in the Holy Ghost"* (Romans 14:17). First, righteousness comes by taking full responsibility for the sin, instead of trying to blame another for it, and confessing it before God (Isaiah 1:18; Ephesians 1:7; I John 1:7). Second, peace comes by forgetting the sin after it has been cleansed (Philippians 3:13; Isaiah 43:18, 19, 25). Third, joy in the Holy Ghost comes by praising God for His forgiveness (Isaiah 44:22, 23; Psalm 107:8).

A woman may also feel guilty about birth control. She needs to make up her mind and settle this matter; the Bible says nothing about it other than the possible reference to the rhythm method in Deuteronomy. It's possible for a woman during 25 years of child-bearing to have a child every ten months (by the way, nursing a child does not prevent conception). If she is going to follow I Corinthians 7:1-5, she needs to use some method of family planning.

Pain. Many women experience pain during the one-flesh relationship; the primary cause for this is lack of lubrication. At certain times of the month and after menopause, lubrication may become inadequate. If this is the case, KY or HR water-soluble surgical jelly should be used. Another cause of such pain may be infections, which can be cured by a doctor's prescription.

Fatigue. When the fatigue level rises, desire diminishes. One study revealed that 10% of the women indicated fatigue as their number one problem in the physical relationship. The average woman needs one more hour's sleep than the average man. Taking an afternoon nap with the kids or lying down after supper helps to refresh the wife. Mothers with preschool children may be especially fatigued and, thus, unable to respond in any way. Hiring adequate help once a week or having a high school girl come in for an hour or two daily to keep the children may provide a terrific boost in the wife's response.

Lack of mood stimulation. As we have pointed

out earlier, women are romantically inclined. They want dim lights, soft music, and a sweet attitude from their husbands. They do not want their work schedule interrupted for love, and they especially react negatively to cutting or belittling remarks and arguments any time during the evening. The husband's help around the house and his aid in getting the children off to bed encourages his wife's attitude toward him.

A woman's hormone cycle. At times during a woman's monthly cycle, she may be very unresponsive, and no amount of technique will make her more responsive. Husbands, therefore, should not expect a response every time.

A lack of proper physical caressing and stimulation. A woman needs ten to thirty minutes of gentle, loving stimulation to prepare her for a pleasurable response. Loving and tender words as well as physical affection go a long way in bringing this eager anticipation on her part.

It is very important to follow the scriptural principles, especially in this one-flesh relationship. Though not the most important thing in marriage, this relationship is the core of ultimate spiritual unity between man and wife. Doing the will of God in any area of life takes work and determination, and this area is no different. Therefore, each couple must determine that they are going to make this one-flesh relationship the unifying, wonderful experience that it should be in a Christ-honoring marriage.

9. Authority and Obedience

A distraught mother I once counseled told me a tale of woe that went something like this: "It's not my two preschoolers, it's two dogs that are driving me crazy. The one is an old hound dog that strayed in one day. The kids felt sorry for him, so we kept him. He's always underfoot, and he drags dead animals into the yard about once a week. I guess I can take him, but I can't stand the thoroughbred my husband bought two years ago when it was a pup. He makes messes all over, chews up any pillow he can get his teeth into, wrecks our furniture, and barks incessantly. I'm ready to crack; I can't take another day."

I suggested first of all that she get rid of one dog, for no mother with preschoolers should have to put up with more than one dog. I then told her that if she decided to keep the thoroughbred she should send it to an obedience school—nothing is worse than a disobedient, unruly dog. She then added, "I also need to send my four-year-old; he seems to be an exact imitation of the dog." My reply to this was a standard one my wife and I give to many parents. I reminded her, "It's your job to train your children. They will act and react as you have trained them in obedience and respect for authority."

Various passages of Scripture teach the necessity for authority and obedience, but the key passage is found in Ephesians 6:1-3, *"Children, obey your parents in the Lord: for this is right. Honour thy father and mother; which is the first commandment with promise; that it may be well with thee, and thou mayest live long on the earth."* Two big questions concerning this passage are, 1) When is a child a child? 2) Is there a difference between obedience and honor?

The Scripture gives insight into the meaning of "child" in the sixth of the Ten Commandments. In this verse, which admonishes children to honor their father and mother, as well as in other scriptural passages teaching this principle, "child" means one who is in the home taking room and board, insurance, and hospitalization and one who is indebted to the parents for his sustenance and livelihood. Although a child is a dependent, a wise parent will train his child to be as independent as possible. He will train the child to take responsibility for his own actions and to begin making his own decisions early—even while the child is still under obligation to his parents.

Concerning the second question, when a child gets out on his own and begins making his own livelihood, he is free from his obligation of obedience but still responsible to honor his parents. He must honor them all of their lives. To honor means to respect, reverence, and be concerned about the one being honored; and though honoring may not include obedience, it can include going to parents for wise counsel when it is needed. Especially since parents have been down the road 20 to 30 years ahead of the child, they probably have made any mistake the child might make.

Parents sometimes forget that they are to train their children in obedience, and that the training contributes to the child's good. The third verse in Ephesians 6, our key passage, refers to Exodus 20:12 which states, *"Honour thy father and thy mother: that thy days may be long upon the land which the Lord thy God giveth thee."* This is the first commandment coupled with a promise, the promise that the child will live to old age if he learns to honor his parents, to obey them during his childhood and his teenage years.

The importance of obedience cannot be over-stressed. In fact, in various places in the Scripture God pronounced severe penalties for any child who did not learn this principle. For example, Exodus 21:15, 17 says, *"And he that smiteth his father, or his mother, shall surely be put to death. And he that curseth his father, or his mother, shall surely be put to death."* God says that if a child strikes or even curses his parents, he should "be put to death." Deuteronomy 21:18-21 is another example. We read, *"If a man have a stubborn and rebellious son, which will not obey the voice of his father, or the voice of his mother, and that, when they have chastened him, will not hearken unto them: then shall his father and his mother lay hold on him, and bring him unto the elders of his city, and unto the gate of his place; And they shall say unto the elders of his city, This our son is stubborn and rebellious, he will not obey our voice; he is a glutton, and a drunkard. And all the men of his city shall stone him with stones, that he die: so shalt thou put evil away from among you; and all Israel shall hear, and fear."* The Israelite child who was rebellious and failed to obey the voice of his parents was to be stoned to death so that all of Israel would hear and fear.

Stoning is a pretty drastic means of disciplining a child, and child-abuse critics would have a royal day in court on any such case. However, these passages show the seriousness of disobedience and rebellion against parents. Though such strong measures are not advocated today, parents still must teach their children this principle of obedience and respect for authority.

The New Testament brings this principle out even more forcefully in I Timothy 6:1-6, which states, *"Let as many servants as are under the yoke count their own masters worthy of all honour, that the name of God and his doctrine be not blasphemed. And they that have believing masters, let them not despise them, because they are brethren; but rather do them service, because they are faithful and beloved, partakers of the benefit. These things teach and exhort. If any man teach otherwise, and consent not to wholesome words, even the words of our Lord Jesus Christ, and to the doctrine which is according to godliness; He is proud, knowing nothing, but doting about questions and strifes of words, whereof cometh envy, strife, railings, evil surmisings, Perverse disputings of men of corrupt minds, and destitute of the truth, supposing that gain is godliness: from such withdraw thyself. But godliness with contentment is great gain."*

The first verse of this passage indicates that a Christian should recognize those in authority and have a servant's attitude toward them. A child may complain that he did not choose his parents or that since his father is a drunk, he shouldn't have to obey him; nonetheless, every child must realize that he has been put into a particular home by God with his future in mind. Proper obedience toward both father and mother is absolutely essential. If the child has a believing father or mother, he should render that parent especially "worthy of honor" since he is faithful, beloved, and protecting toward his child.

Children ought to be aware of authority in other areas of life as well. The policeman on the corner, the teacher in the classroom, the principal, the employer are all authority figures and should be respected. The servant attitude of obedience established in the home is the foundation for all other types of relationship to authority. Consequently, if respect for authority is properly adhered to in the home, it will also be adhered to outside the home. A well-trained child will have much less difficulty in life and will cause his parents much less heartache.

The second verse of I Timothy 6 further states that these principles should not only be taught but also exhorted. Even children ought to exhort their brothers, sisters and playmates to obey authority figures. Verses 3-5 of this chapter go on to describe the disobedient and rebellious person and admonishes the Christian to withdraw himself from anyone who displays this disobedient attitude and refuses to heed authority. Finally, verse 6 reminds the Christian that godly people are content; and by contrast he may assume that those who are ungodly, who resist authority, are discontent and unhappy. Consequently, by teaching the authority principle in the home, parents are helping their child toward a happy, contented life.

This training is more, however, than just simple conditioning. A child has a mind, and even when he is two years old, his attitudes can be directed toward respect for authority. Conditioning, such as approval or spanking, should be coupled with an explanation and an insistence that the child make up his mind to do right. This type of training involves applying several principles.

Making sure the child knows which authority he is to obey. Too many bosses, such as aunts, grandmothers, older brothers and sisters, can be confusing—especially if they don't all agree. Every child needs to know that his parents are in agreement concerning his life and benefits from a united front in any commands, decisions, and responses. When the child asks an important question, he doesn't need an instant decision. Waiting until the next morning to give him an answer allows the parents time to talk over the facts. Children have a sly way of playing one parent against another and actually driving a wedge between them. The wise parent never sides with the child against the spouse.

Following through on the decisions made. Respect for authority breaks down if parents do not follow up on the decision and make certain that commands are carried out. Disrespect and disobedience should be punished with authority and firmness, but anger should not be part of the punishment.

Setting an example. It is easy to make rules and standards, but more difficult to enforce them. Children respect consistency in their parents, for it enhances the authority. The rule given today should be the same rule the children are expected to obey tomorrow.

Taking time and patience to train children. The

key is continual guidance every day in the kind of behavior expected. Since children forget very easily, they must be gently reminded and at times even retaught.

Balancing discipline with love. A study of schizophrenic Christians found that these people had invariably had stern, unyielding, letter-of-the-law parents who punished without love. The parents were more concerned about the violation of the rule than properly training the child—more concerned about the offense than about remedying the action of the offender and restoring him to freedom from guilt.

Training a child to respect authority will lay the basis for a well-adjusted life and future happiness, and the result is worth all the effort that parents put forth.

10   Balanced Discipline

"Stop that!"

"Get away from there!"

"I've told you a hundred times today to pick that up."

"This is your third spanking today."

"Wait till your father gets home; he'll take care of you."

Are these examples of a bad child, or do they also illustrate a parent's lack of knowledge about how to handle children? What are some good techniques that have worked for other Christian families? What is the biblical view of discipline for today's Christian parent?

Part of balanced discipline is punishing a child when he does wrong. Most Christian parents know such Bible verses as *"He that spareth his rod hateth his son: but he that loveth him chasteneth him betimes"* (Proverbs 13:24); *"Chasten thy son while there is hope, and let not thy soul spare for his crying"* (Proverbs 19:18); *"Foolishness is bound in the heart of a child; but the rod of correction shall drive it far from him"* (Proverbs 22:15); and *"Withold not correction from the child: for if thou beatest him with the rod, he shall not die"* (Proverbs 23:13). These verses stress the corrective aspect of discipline, which is indeed important in training a child. Children must be aware of the consequences of sin, and punishment is in order for going beyond the established boundary lines, directly disobeying authority, or deliberately infringing upon the rights of others. (Application of these principles to the very young child is in Chapters 12 and 13.)

Our rules should also be simple and enforceable; they should be properly interpreted to the children by simple explanation and sufficient examples. Appropriate punishment—such as spanking, making the child go to his room or taking away privileges (such as watching television, using a bike, or going to a special place or event)—helps children to get into the habit of avoiding inappropriate behavior. (Of course, a parent should never punish a child for an accident, and he needs to make every effort to help his child do right.)

There is, however, another important, yet neglected part of discipline. This is the approach given in Proverbs 25:11, *"A word fitly spoken is like apples of gold in pictures of silver."* Ninety-five percent of what children do during the waking day is acceptable behavior; yet, in the name of training, parents often concentrate on the five percent of unacceptable behavior to the exclusion of supporting and encouraging the children's good behavior. Proverbs 3:27 admonishes believers to *"Withold not good [or help] from them to whom it is due, when it is in the power of thine hand to do it."* According to Proverbs 15:23, *"A man hath joy by the answer of his mouth: and a word spoken in due season, how good is it!"*

Parents should concentrate on being as positive as possible with their children. A nod of the head, a smile, or a verbal encouragement indicates support, acceptance, and approval. This part of discipline does not conflict with the punishment aspect. II Timothy 4:2 teaches that as we give the Word to our children, in season and out of season, we should "reprove, rebuke, and exhort with all longsuffering and doctrine." This verse indicates both sides of discipline: *reprove* means "to convict or convince"; *rebuke* means "to charge a child to follow certain behavior or to demand restitution for error"; *exhort* means "to comfort, encourage, or beseech"; and *longsuffering* indicates "a calm spirit and a gentle teaching (of doctrine)." Parents of teenage children and parents whose children are in Christian work testify that balanced discipline has provided the atmosphere for fewer problems and for the continued spiritual growth of the children.

Christians should be motivated to do things that are acceptable to the Lord by the inner satisfaction which comes from pleasing Him. Young children, however, find this a very hard concept to grasp in their day-to-day activities, and they can be assisted in comprehending this idea by receiving encouragement from their parents. For this reason occasional rewards are vital to balanced discipline. Rewards can consist of many things: a simple nod of approval, a verbal compliment, a word of agreement or encouragement, a hug, a pat on the back, a smile with a touch of the hand. Sometimes a parent can offer material things such as a new toy or material for a treehouse, a fishing trip with Dad, or a shopping trip and lunch downtown with Mother. These times of rewarding can be a tremendous time of fellowship for the father and son or mother and daughter.

Immediately, some parents may say, "That sounds like bribery, and children have to learn to do good without getting any kind of reward. Rewards have no place in Christianity." Don't they? The Christian's main reward in heaven for his good works here on earth will be Christ's *"Well done, thou good and faithful servant,"* and crowns will also be part of his reward.

In Proverbs 13:19 we read, *"The desire accomplished is sweet to the soul."* Solomon recognized the reward of accomplishment. How often has someone been asked, "Why are you doing that?" only to reply, "Because it is so rewarding." When he makes such a reply, a person is not talking about money, but rather the inner satisfaction of having made a worthwhile contribution. Children also need to learn this kind of motivation, but it is not an attitude they develop quickly. Preschool children need short-term goals with more immediate, often tangible rewards. Children who have been discipline problems also need short-term goals and rewards until they can establish a better pattern of behavior. As the child learns to set goals for positive behavior, he gains satisfaction from accomplishing the desired end.

Along with rewards, children need verbal encouragement as part of balanced discipline. Parents should avoid falling into a pattern of harping, nagging, or attacking the character of the child. Such comments as "You must be stupid to do a trick like that" or "Why are you so stubborn and rebellious?" or "You'll be the death of me yet" or "You're hopeless" tend to tear down the self-image and defeat the child's spirit. Ephesians 6:4 and Colossians 3:21 tell us not to scold or nag our children so much that they become angry, resentful, and discouraged, but rather give them suggestions and godly advice. Real Christian training should be supportive and should build up the child's self-image; that is, it should make the child feel that he is responsible for his behavior and that he is capable of making good decisions—wise choices that lead to behavior acceptable to his parents and to God.

Children need comfort, encouragement, and support. David laments in Psalm 69:20, *"Reproach hath broken my heart; I am full of heaviness: and I looked for some to take pity, but there was none; and for comforters, but I found none."* A number of children in good Christian homes need comfort and encouragement rather than the uncontrolled, heavy hand. Isaiah 50:4 says, *"The Lord God hath given me the tongue of the learned, that I should know how to speak a word in season to him that is weary: he wakeneth mine ear to hear as the learned."*

Many mothers have asked us how they can handle an unruly child. One of the first things we have them do is see how many times a day they rebuke the child and how many times they reward and praise him. Proverbs 16:24 says, *"Pleasant words are as an honeycomb, sweet to the soul, and health to the bones."* Also, how many times does the mother say—and mean—"I love you"? A child needs to know that he is loved whether his behavior is good or bad. Often parents of unruly children give all rebuke and no reward. It is not the lack of punishment, but often the overuse of it without any positive, loving encouragement that causes the difficulty (for example, the earlier example in chapter nine concerning the study done on Christians who were schizophrenic).

When discipline is coupled with verbal encouragement, it can even prevent misbehavior. Many times parents can anticipate problems or trouble, and a gentle reminder, removing the temptation or talking with the child about the dangers inherent in a situation will eliminate or minimize the temptation. For example, children should be told that everyone is tempted to steal (I Corinthians 10:13) and that stores have elaborate systems to detect shoplifters. Then parents teach their children how to avoid all appearance of evil (I Thessalonians 5:22) by not picking up things in a store unless the item is to be purchased. Similarly, parents can specify exactly what kind of behavior is expected at Grandmother's house before going to visit. If parents take the time beforehand to train, they will not have to take the time afterward to punish.

Discipline actually means training. In a given situation, whether training is primarily correction or encouragement depends on the child, the situation, what has gone before, and what is to follow (these principles will be discussed in more detail in later chapters). The love of the Lord and the leading of the Holy Spirit will help parents know whether they are giving their children the right proportions of both kinds of discipline.

Parents who give their children punishment *only* are doing a great deal of damage to them and are not adhering to Scripture and the direction of the Holy Spirit. Training and love should always follow punishment if it is to be effective. An unruly and unmanageable child may be the parents' own fault, even though they may want to blame heredity, physical difficulties, and bad companions. A balanced, biblical approach to training, however, can help even a problem child become a joy to his family and to others who know him.

11   Father's Big Responsibility

It seems that everyone knows a pastor, deacon, missionary, or stalwart Christian layman whose child is a spiritual failure. Why? Can parents prevent such mistakes? Yes, there is a success formula for spiritual education that can help with this problem. After establishing the necessity of discipline, parents should concentrate on who should administer such discipline and how it should be administered. The key to avoiding the problems of wayward children is found in the father who lovingly trains his children to make the right decisions—this kind of father can be assured of his children's success. *"Fathers, provoke not your children to wrath: but bring them up in the nurture and admonition of the Lord"* (*Ephesians 6:4*). This verse is the mandate from God to fathers not to provoke, but train.

A father who becomes upset or unreasonable when dealing with his child will inevitably provoke the child to wrath. When such unfavorable reactions and provocations become the habitual method of discipline, only discouragement, anger, bitterness, and rebellion result. A recent survey of students who harbored bad feelings about their fathers confirmed this fact. The students listed five main things which aggravated these ill feelings: 1) the father was always critical and seldom offered praise; 2) the father could never admit he was wrong; 3) he had no time to listen to his children; 4) he used degrading terms to refer to the children such as "that stupid kid"; 5) he compared the children in a negative manner.

On the other hand, research indicates that fathers who have a high degree of *control* over their children and also exhibit a great amount of *love*, interest, and involvement produce children who possess a good self-concept, obey authority, and follow the parents' life style. When either the control or the love is missing, however, there is the possibility of a problem child. Paul said in I Thessalonians 2:11 that he *"exhorted and comforted and charged every one of you, as a father doth his children,"* indicating the necessity of love as well as training.

This necessary fatherly love can best be generated by letting the Holy Spirit fill the father's life. For the fruit of the Spirit that will result in his life will also produce the ingredients of true fatherly love. This love is also the foundation for training children in making the five important spiritual decisions that are the bases for the child's right actions.

Accepting salvation. The world believes that salvation is obtained by works such as joining a church, getting baptized, giving to charity, reforming outward behavior, or a variety of other means people use to try to gain favor with God. The Bible says, however, in Isaiah 64:6 *"All our righteousnesses are as filthy rags."* Ephesians 2:8, 9 also says, *"For by grace are*

*ye saved through faith, and that not of yourselves: it is the gift
of God: Not of works, lest any man should boast."*

To be saved, or born again, one must believe certain things about Jesus Christ. First, he must realize that Jesus Christ is God and is the only begotten Son of God. Second, he must realize that God loved him enough to come down to earth to suffer, bleed, and die for his sins. John 3:17, *"For God sent not his son into the world to condemn the world: but that the world through him might be saved."* Christ's purpose for coming to earth was not to live a perfect, sinless life condemning others by his example, but He came for the sole purpose of shedding His blood on Calvary as payment for men's sins. Third, Christ was buried and rose again the third day for men's justification. Everyone must believe these things in order to be saved.

He must take one further step, however, before he can obtain the salvation found in Revelation 3:20, *"Behold, I stand at the door, and knock: if any man hear my voice, and open the door, I will come in to him, and will sup with him, and he with me,"* and John 1:12, *"But as many as received him, to them gave he power to become the sons of God, even to them that believe on his name."* There must be a time when he asks Christ to come into his heart—a time when he receives Christ as his personal Saviour, Colossians 1:27, *"To whom God would make known what is the riches of the glory of this mystery among the Gentiles: which is Christ in you, the hope of glory."* Salvation is turning from his sins to Christ and accepting Him into his life by faith. The moment a person does so he is saved; Christ immediately gives him eternal life. He becomes part of Him, and the believer is said to be in Christ (II Corinthians 5:17), and he becomes a partaker of Christ's divine nature.

The Holy Spirit comes into a person's heart the same time he accepts Christ to comfort and empower him to do great things through Christ. The decision to accept Christ and the indwelling of the Holy Spirit will not completely eliminate all sin, but it will completely eliminate the condemnation for sins (Romans 8:1). A Christian can be assured that his sins—past, present, and future—have been paid for, washed white as snow by the blood of Christ.

When a Christian does sin following salvation he hurts his fellowship with Christ and needs to confess his wrongdoing (I John 1:9). He need not, however, struggle through life working to maintain righteousness before God; instead he lives by faith, trusts Christ as Saviour, and looks to His Word for guidance and direction in his daily walk with Him.

Studying the Word. The second main decision Christians need to make is the decision to accept the authority of God's Word and to study it regularly. This principle includes memorizing Scripture. I Peter 2:2, 3 says that the way newborn Christians grow is by drinking the milk of the Word (studying and learning the basic doctrines of God's Word). Later, as they become stronger, they begin to get into the meat of the Word, i.e., the harder, more difficult passages. Psalm 119 specifically indicates that studying and memorizing the Word of God will be beneficial (Psalm 119:9, 11). Why? Because God's Word never changes; it lasts eternally (Isaiah 40:8, Psalm 119:89 and Hebrews 4:12). It will prove powerful in the lives of all who apply it.

One formula for applying the Word of God is the 4M formula of Psalm 119:9, 11, 15, 17;   1) mark se-

lected Scriptures; 2) memorize these selected pas-
sages; 3) meditate upon them; 4) master them.
All Christians should have some kind of plan for
Scripture memorization (be it only a verse a week).
Memorizing God's Word does more to change a per-
son's life than probably any other one thing.

A good book to help young Christians begin to
grasp God's working through the ages is Larkin's
book *Dispensational Truth*. It contains many charts
that chronologically illustrate difficult portions of
Scripture such as Daniel and Revelation.

In line with learning God's Word, a young person
going to college should go to a college where the
Bible is thoroughly studied. Most good Christian
colleges require Bible courses each semester and also
provide additional Bible electives to aid a young person in attaining a firm grasp of the Scriptures. If
God's Word is to be his guide throughout life and
his authority in matters of faith and practice, a
Christian must know it well.

Separating from worldliness. God's holiness
demands that a Christian separate himself from sin
and corruption and anything else that hurts the
Gospel. A Christian is to live a holy life. He must
decide (an act of the will) to put off the old man
with its lusts and corruption; and, through the daily
renewing of his mind, *"put on the new man, which after
God is created in righteousness and true holiness" (Ephesians
4:24)*.

A Christian has to be *in* the world in order to
reach the world, but he is warned not to become
part *of* the world. II Corinthians 6:14-16 says specifically *"Be ye not unequally yoked together with unbelievers: for
what fellowship hath righteousness with unrighteousness: and*

what communion hath light with darkness? And what concord hath Christ with Belial? Or what part hath he that believeth with an infidel? And what agreement hath the temple of God with idols? For ye are the temple of the living God: as God hath said, I will dwell in them, and walk in them; and I will be their God and they shall be my people."

Since his body is the temple of the Holy Ghost, since he is bought with a price, a Christian is to glorify God in his body and spirit daily (I Corinthians 6:19, 20). This glorification involves a sacrifice of self and the flesh. It is an attitude of the mind—a daily agreement to separate himself unto God. II Corinthians 6:17, 18 states, *"Wherefore come out from among them, and be ye separate, saith the Lord, and touch not the unclean thing; and I will receive you, and will be a Father unto you, and ye shall be my sons and daughters, saith the Lord Almighty."* When a Christian separates himself unto God he allows the Holy Spirit to lead and direct in his everyday decisions regarding holiness.

A Christian ought to be fully aware of the unholy trinity (the world, the flesh, and the Devil) who make attacks against his spiritual life (Ephesians 2:2, 3). They act against his godly nature in their effort to mar his testimony and Gospel witness and in hopes that he will resign himself to living a defeated Christian life.

Young people have to learn that they must be very careful whom they associate with in organizations, in dating, in social activities, and in general life style. It is imperative that a young person not date (or marry) an unsaved person, but choose his friends carefully and have biblical convictions on the matters of dress, activities, and music. He should be aware of the scriptural prohibition concerning joining certain organizations with the unsaved such as lodges, unions, and various other associations where the ungodly will affect or control his beliefs or life style. He also needs to discern and avoid religious groups that fail to follow scriptural teachings regarding doctrine and religious practice (Galatians 1:9).

The Devil will also try to use current fads, customs, and music to try to enmesh a Christian in worldly habits and desires. It may be a terrific struggle for a Christian to gain victory over these habits, but the secret in obtaining such a victory is to concentrate on loving Christ and His Word and decide against the world and its short-lived pleasures (I John 2:15, 16; Hebrews 11:25).

There are three basic components of the term "world" as we have been using it. One aspect is the lust of the flesh—the sensual, bodily pleasures which allure people into all types of sexual sins, gluttony, and corrupt habits. Second is the lust of the eyes—making people discontent with their social and financial positions. This sin causes them to be materialistic and to view material gain as the ultimate criterion for success. The third aspect, the pride of life, brings about vain glory and selfishness. These three are worldly pleasures that every Christian has to fight. In doing so, it is good to check to make sure that he is doing what is right. A good test is to ask the following questions: Will it hurt me (I Corinthians 6:19, 20)? Will it hurt others (I Corinthians 8:9, 13)? Will it hurt my Spirit-filled testimony for Jesus Christ (I Corinthians 9:19-23 and Romans 14:23)? Will I be doing it to the glory of God (I Corinthians 10:31)? God desires that every Christian have an abundant life. He can experience such a life by doing God's will and following the leadership of His Spirit through His Word.

Surrendering to Christ. There comes a time in every Christian's life when the Holy Spirit presses him to surrender or dedicate his life completely, unreservedly to Jesus Christ. A few people take this step at salvation, but most Christians make this decision at another time in their lives. It is, however, more than laying a stick in the fire at a campfire meeting or volunteering to become a missionary. It is a time when a person is really willing to follow Romans 12:1, 2 *"I beseech you therefore, brethren, by the mercies of God, that ye present your bodies a living sacrifice, holy, acceptable unto God, which is your reasonable service. And be not conformed to this world: but be ye transformed by the renewing of your mind, that ye may prove what is that good, and acceptable, and perfect, will of God."* It is the start of a crucified life (Galatians 2:20) when a person decides to deny self and the flesh daily (Luke 9:23) and to yield completely to the leadership of the Holy Spirit (Ephesians 5:11-20).

The resulting behavior of the Spirit-filled life is the fruit of the Spirit mentioned in Galatians 5:22, 23. Prayer becomes a natural, daily contact and closeness with God, not a time of introspection or public confession or a speaking in tongues or any other wildfire action.

Neither are there any degrees of the infilling of the Holy Spirit. It is simply a matter of being yielded to the Spirit's control or not being yielded at any given moment. A person who has surrendered his life to God and who daily lives a crucified life is prepared to go into the ministry, to the mission field, or any of the other various forms of Christian service the Lord may call him into. It is merely a question of acknowledging God in every matter in order that He may direct his path (Proverbs 3:5, 6).

Often a Christian goes through life not really knowing the purpose and fullness that the Holy Spirit can provide because he does not reckon himself dead and buried with Christ that he may bring forth fruit. John 12:24, 25 states, *"Verily, verily, I say unto you, Except a corn of wheat fall into the ground and die, it abideth alone: but if it die, it bringeth forth much fruit. He that loveth his life shall lose it; and he that hateth his life in this world shall keep it unto life eternal."*

A Spirit-filled Christian manifesting the fruit of the Spirit characterizes the surrendered person. He seems to have power in his ministry, witnessing, and daily living. He doesn't ask silly questions about whether to tithe before or after taxes or if it is all right to watch movies on television, etc., for he has the discernment and the guidance of the Holy Spirit to show him all things (John 16:13). His dedicated attitude eliminates these inane and superfluous questions.

One reason for so much nastiness in Christianity is that too many carnal Christians react to other carnal Christians making everyone upset. God desires Spirit-filled Christians who are truly loving people presenting godly testimonies wherever they go.

Soulwinning. Every Christian needs to decide he is going to take part in carrying out the great commission. This includes a gamut of opportunities from passing out tracts, witnessing to friends, street preaching, jail visitation, holding Bible classes, door-to-door visitation and child evangelism to eventually becoming a missionary, pastor, Christian school teacher, or other full-time Christian worker.

A person who has made the soulwinning decision will view people either as lost, hell-bound sinners or as saints who need discipling and building up in the faith. He observes the larger picture—the picture beyond the growth of a Sunday school class, a bus route, or even a church and sees the world in need of the Saviour. He will constantly do all he can to get the Gospel message to sinners. He will prepare by carrying tracts, by memorizing good salvation verses and by being alert to the opportunities the Holy Spirit gives him. Every Christmas card, conversation with a stranger, and contact with lost neighbors and friends will contain a Gospel witness. Lost loved ones and relatives will be won, and fellow workers and business associates will be brought into contact with the Gospel following this initial soulwinning decision.

II Corinthians 5:11-21 gives some of the reasons that compel a man to constant soulwinning. Knowing the terror of the Lord and experiencing the constraining love of Christ will cause a Spirit-filled Christian to persuade men to *turn* to Christ before they *burn* eternally. Psalm 126:5, 6 gives a tried and proven formula for winning souls.

It is especially important that a father make these five decisions and then train his children to do so. Studies show that the absence of the father (or of his influence) contributes to his children's (particularly sons') low motivation for achievement, their need for immediate gratification at the expense of long range benefits, their low self-esteem, and an unusual susceptibility to peer group influence.

A father's habitually carrying out these principles

in his own life can be an effective influence on his whole family. The father is responsible for regular family devotions and getting his family to church, revival meetings, camps, seminars, and Christian schools so that the family is properly trained. Finding time to teach and practice these principles is essential and is a crucial factor in most Christians' lives. Everyone finds time for the things he deems important (for example, most fathers seem to feel that television is important, for they average 28 hours per week). Sports and business also rank high on most fathers' top priority list, but the rearing of a family for Christ is the father's main thrust in life. Every father has much training to do, and he needs the help of the Lord to give him strength, wisdom, and power. He needs to take the same vow Joshua took in the Old Testament: *"As for me and my house, we will serve the Lord"* *(Joshua 24:15).*

12 Principles for Building Up Children for God

Guiding children successfully is perhaps the greatest desire of parents. Certain basic principles can serve as guidelines in child-training in five basic areas.

Understanding a child's uniqueness. Each child is a unique individual and should be helped to develop as an individual. Parents and teachers should be cautioned not to compare children or to try to make them fit into the mold of some other child. Nor can parents relive their lives through their children. Dad may have wished to become a football star, but his 135-pound, 6-foot, 15-year-old cannot fulfill this lost dream.

A good parent should think in terms of helping each child to develop to his individual potential. God has made us each unique; Psalm 139:13, 14 states, *"For thou hast possessed my reins: thou hast covered me in my mother's womb. I will praise thee; for I am fearfully and wonderfully made: marvellous are thy works; and that my soul knoweth right well."*

James Dobson, in his book *Hide or Seek*, points out the world's false criteria for judging a child. The world's standards set up beauty and intelligence as the highest priority. Money and athletic prowess become important also as the child grows older. God, however, has a different standard: character, spirituality, and right attitudes are the qualities that God favors. If parents emphasize these characteristics they can help their children develop in their unique God-given way.

Parents need to be willing to listen and to be aware of their child's individual viewpoint and consider his ideas. When a child is ready to talk, it's important for parents to be available and to react with enthusiasm to his exciting news such as finding a bird's nest, coming in third in the spelling bee, having an art paper hung in the classroom, or making a score at the ball game. They should conversely not overreact when a child tells them about a problem; they need to be careful not to make a major crisis out of a minor incident. For example, some parents overreact against the child when he has been reprimanded at school, or others overreact against the authority who has done the correcting—either is wrong. Either overreaction against the child or overprotection of him will lead to problems. Children need loving, firm, understanding guidance from their parents.

Parents should respond to their children's emotional individuality. Children all have the same basic emotions and all go through similar stages, but each child tends to manifest his emotions in a different way. As parents recognize this, they can help their children properly handle their anger, fear, hostility, and later their sexual emotions. Natural emotions need to be properly channeled. To an infant the emotion of love is initially conveyed through the warmth of handling, kissing, rocking, and touching. The trust which results from these initial manifestations begins to develop love. Later on, the parents' example of giving and meeting needs demonstrates the broader concept of God's love. The child should learn to use his emotions to glorify God; he should be taught to subject emotional impulses to basic standards, beliefs, and principles. He needs to understand that he should not wait for an emotional feeling to do what he ought to do, but he should do what is right at the appropriate time whether he feels like it or not. Proverbs 20:11 says, *"Even a child is known by his doings, whether his work be pure, and whether it be right."*

Running an efficient household. A household should be organized for efficiency. Bedtime, getting-up time, bed-making, meal times, cleaning time—all of these should be areas in which the children can help. "Many hands make light work"—this principle applied to family life can also increase family unity. One mother listed the monthly household jobs on slips of paper; each Saturday morning her three girls drew one of the slips and did the job listed while the mother worked at other household tasks and the father and son worked outside. When all had completed their work, they would celebrate with a special noon lunch or picnic.

Another aid to efficiency is to have "a place for everything and everything in its place." Little children especially need a specific place for the things they use daily such as scissors, tape, crayons, and paper. They also need to be taught to put things away immediately when they are finished with them. For example, when they come in from school in the afternoon they should place their books on their desks, hang their coats in the closet, and put their school clothes away after changing into play clothes.

Goal setting is another means toward efficiency. Daily, weekly, monthly, and yearly goals can be very helpful, and writing goals out can also be a good idea. Human beings get a sense of satisfaction and accomplishment when they see goals reached (Proverbs 13:19). Goals also help children to discipline themselves; they teach children not to procrastinate, but to do what they ought to do when they ought to do it. Daily responsibilities also develop good habits. For example, caring for a household pet, doing daily chores, running a paper route, practicing music, and memorizing Scripture verses are some of the tangible goals a child can fulfill daily.

Building character by proper training. A child learns most by example. *"As is the mother so is her daughter" (Ezekiel 16:44).* What parents say is reinforced or contradicted by what they do. A mother who pays back the supermarket clerk the excess change she gave her shows the child, by her honesty in the situation, what she has been trying to teach him.

Children also learn to love others through the parents' example. Loving others is a result of truly loving God; for love for God is manifested by an outreach to others. Helping a widowed mother with her children, making a meal for a sick family, and sharing a gift of Florida oranges are all ways to let children see love in action.

Even though II Corinthians 12:14 states that

"children ought not to lay up for the parents but the parents for the children," a fortunate child also learns how to work. A life of ease and pleasure-seeking is an empty and meaningless existence, but a child can experience the thrill of accomplishment by earning his own money. Children must be taught early that creature comforts do not produce themselves; they are produced by hard work. The ownership of property is the motivation for work, and people must own before they are able to give. Children will not become materialistic and selfish if, along with the principle of work and earning, they are taught the joy of giving.

Parents should not take the grit out of their children's lives by protecting them from every hardship, blow, or disappointment. Remember, adversity strengthens character. For example, instead of car pooling, children could walk or ride bikes to school. This extra effort will enable them to see and enjoy nature, opportunities they would miss looking out of a car window. Having them face the elements (rain, ice, and snow) while on a paper route will give them a strengthened will to face difficult times later in life. One mother thought she was helping her son, 13 years old, by getting up every morning at 5 a.m. to take him on his paper route. She was actually harming him by not letting him fulfill his own responsibilities. Children are resilient; they can take a lot if Mother doesn't make them feel abused and neglected by an overly sympathetic attitude. Such a statement as, "Oh, honey, it's so cold out there; I'm afraid you'll freeze on your paper route," produces a negative attitude in the mind of the child. Mother ought to say, "When you finish your paper route, I'll have a hot cup of chocolate waiting and a good breakfast."

Parents can also help their children use the usual times of aimlessness or loafing as times of training. They should have a number of different job experiences to train them for future full-time service. Summer jobs can help children acquire certain useful skills. Those preparing for the mission field should know something about carpentry, auto mechanics, money handling, and record keeping. Song leading, playing a musical instrument, and child evangelism work can also be advantageous. All of the skills just mentioned can be developed through various summer jobs, Christian camps, businesses, etc. The right part-time job during school can also be beneficial—jobs such as babysitting, maintenance work, sales work, or waitressing.

Training children to have a positive faith attitude. Everyone needs to keep a cheerful, positive attitude in the home. Ephesians 5:19 speaks of being Spirit-filled Christians, *"Speaking to yourselves in psalms and hymns and spiritual songs, singing and making melody in your heart to the Lord."* Parents should live daily as though it were the last time they would be with their family, for the joy of the Lord should be evident in their homes more than any other place. The home is where Christianity proves itself to the child.

The family needs a cooperative spirit, fostering an attitude to help one another overcome sins and temptations. A wife's greatest problem is likely to be rebellion toward her husband. A husband could help by being the loving and sensitive husband he ought to be. For the husband, lust may pose the greatest temptation. The wife, of course, can help in this area by taking care of her husband's physical needs and making the intimate relationship what it ought to be. For most children, disobedience may be the greatest sin-problem. Consistent parents who agree and who balance their punishment with love will help in this area.

Christian parents should fight negative attitudes through positive approval, by solving problems rather than placing blame and by looking at God's blessings rather than at the difficulties. Using "next time" instead of "if only" in times of defeat and disappointment can also bring about a dynamic spirit of improvement. Contentment is basic to a positive attitude, and children must be taught to praise God for the pleasurable as well as the difficult times of life.

It's important to accentuate children's successes and to minimize their failures. Parents can find things daily to compliment them about, being careful not to overemphasize mistakes, failures, or accidents. Proverbs 12:25 admonishes Christians concerning this principle, *"Heaviness in the heart of a man maketh it stoop: but a good word maketh it glad."*

A child wants attention; if he cannot obtain it by behaving properly, he will attain it by misbehaving. One little four-year-old girl was placed in a day care center while her mother worked all day teaching first grade in the same school. The little girl started taking off her clothes, pulling over bookcases, spilling trays of juice, etc. Each time she did so, the principal sent for her mother, and the little girl obtained the attention she had been wanting. Her antics were merely a cry for mother's attention. She should have been having this need fulfilled from someone at home during the day instead of being placed in the nursery. Children who do not get approval from both parents are especially susceptible to peer influence. A good teacher, youth director, or relative can serve as a substitute parent with a widow's children, helping them to gain the necessary attention and approval.

Children tend to react to their parents' basic attitudes. Positive attitudes usually indicate real faith and trust in God. Christians who manifest genuine faith are usually very positive people, and their children have the same positive faith attitudes.

Maintaining a balance between training, control, and correction. Discipline is more than punishment. It is the balance between training, control, and correction, and it is essential for a child's proper growth.

Training is helping children to recognize and respect the boundaries of any situation. These boundary lines should be tight when the child is young, but they may expand as he grows and matures. At age two, he's not allowed to go out of the yard or to cross the street unattended. By ten these boundaries have changed, as have many other restrictions.

It's best to think in terms of general principles rather than specific rules. In training, four general principles are applicable in all situations:

1. Being constructive instead of destructive.

2. Respecting the rights of others.

3. Following standard operating procedures, whether it be how to line up at camp, for dinner, or how to pass papers in class. The standard operating procedure can be any procedure that the parent, teacher, or leader desires the child to follow in any particular situation.

4. Doing the will of God by knowing Bible Action Truths (see Appendix) and by applying them to daily living.

Little children forget very easily and must be constantly reminded of these general principles. Everyday situations can adequately illustrate these principles; for example, the constructive nature of building a snowman rather than kicking down those that others have made.

Control is providing the conditions for right action. Children generally respond correctly when they have the conditions conducive to right action. The Devil, the flesh, and the world (Ephesians 2:2-3) will give the Christian child real trouble, but parents can minimize these influences by providing conditions which will motivate good behavior.

Children need an environment of positive acceptance and encouragement; they profit much from positive attention. But both positive and negative control work, and there should be a balance between the two.

A child's dynamic energies should be channeled into constructive activity. Television viewing is passive rather than active participation and for the most part provides no outlet for energy. It provides instead a worldly, corrupt, and emotionally overwhelming environment for the child. Creative play is much more beneficial, for it provides for both the physical and imaginative outlet.

Correction is providing remedial action when a child goes beyond the boundary lines established. Spanking is very effective, if done properly and not in anger. There are also other effective methods such as withholding privileges, verbal reprimands, isolating the child for a short period, (ten minutes for children under eight years old) and letting him take the consequences of his wrong actions. Punishment should be given soon after the offense (Ecclesiastes 8:11); in serious offenses, however, a mother may want to wait until her husband comes home to handle the situation.

It is easy to fall into the trap of nagging. Parents who constantly use "never" and "always" are nagging. Instead, command or instruction should be clear and have a time limit, possibly followed by a gentle reminder. Then if the child does not obey within the time limit, he should be punished. Once the parents enforce a punishment, they should leave the matter, never bringing up past sins and errors. The basic attitude is always, "I love you whether you're good or bad, but when you're bad, it makes me very sad." Praying with the child after punishment is helpful.

Balance in these three aspects of discipline is vital. It takes time, especially in the early years. If a mother works 40 hours a week, her additional household duties don't allow her the time necessary for proper training and control. Consequently, her discipline of the children becomes a series of up-setting events which call for a great deal of punishment. This can be discouraging to a child and may cause problems rather than remedying the situation. There needs to be a consistent balanced emphasis.

As early as two years of age a child can be taught to make up his mind to do right. A bad or evil action is the result of a decision at some time to go in the wrong direction, and children can allow bad actions to become habitual. Correction can help them make up their minds to reverse or change their behavior. But love must balance out punishment if it is to be truly effective.

13   Then They Turned Two

Discipline is always a full-time job, but there usually comes a time in every mother's life when she feels especially discouraged about her child-training ability. This time most often comes when the first child reaches about the age of two. Mothers continually complain that two-year-olds are impossible and that they see no way to retain their sanity if the child persists in his obstreperous behavior.

The two-year-old stage is a time of emotional disequilibrium. The child does not know why he acts or feels as he does. Mothers complain of several typical symptoms:

1. The child is constantly into everything.
2. The child's behavior is erratic. He can be angelic one minute and impossible the next. He creates scenes at the worst possible moments and is unpredictable. Consequently, parents hesitate to take the child out to church or any other social activity that necessitates quiet behavior for any length of time.
3. The child is stubborn, rebellious, and given to temper tantrums when he does not get his way.
4. The child is noisy, talkative and asks a thou-

sand questions daily.

5. The child doesn't want to go to bed and refuses to stay in bed once he is there. In the middle of the night the child comes into the parents' bedroom because he is supposedly afraid.

The following suggestions are helpful in dealing with these normal problems of the two-year-old and can serve as a foundation for rearing children through the formative years.

Anticipating the stage the child is in. The two-year-old goes through a negative stage when he is exerting his will and testing boundaries. During this time firm boundary lines are important, and the child must be trained to be submissive and to obey authority.

Since this is a negative stage, parents need to give as few "no's" and commands as possible. The fewer the commands, the fewer the opportunities for violation. For instance, if in a relaxing moment a parent wants his child to sit on his lap, he shouldn't make the request a command that the child might react against. For then the parent has a difficult time insisting that his child obey such a command. If it really doesn't matter, the parent might suggest, "Son, how would you like to sit on Dad's lap?" This request will give the child a chance to develop the ability to make decisions by saying either yes or no. He may be thinking about playing with a particular toy at the time of the request. But the choice should be his in a matter such as this.

However, when a parent asks questions in which the child has no real choice, he shouldn't expect a yes answer. In such cases if the child responds negatively and the parent insists that he respond positively, he will begin to exert his stubbornness and rebellion. For example, asking a child if he wants to go to bed can create a hassle since he must go whether he wants to or not.

We talked with one mother who was having severe problems with a rebellious child. After observing the way she handled him, we found that she continually posed questions to him such as, "Would you like to eat now?" "Would you like to get in the car and come with me?" His immediate answers were the inevitable "no," and the trouble started when the mother had to convince him to do what he had to do in the first place. You should talk to a child in positive command terms when dealing with inevitable things, i.e., "We are going to bed as soon as you put your toys away."

Training the child in obedience. One of the main biblical principles concerning child-training is obedience to authority. This training should start when the child is between one and two years. Ephesians 6:1 says, *"Children, obey your parents in the Lord: for this is right."* Verses two and three go on to say that longevity is a reward for such behavior. A rebellious child has a serious problem, for God hates the sin of rebellion. If a child rebels against his parents, he will eventually rebel against civil and divine authority. Early training in obedience prepares the child to obey God and all authority God will place over him later.

The idea that defiance in one- or two-year-olds is merely a stage and should be ignored is unscriptural. Though most children do pass through a stage in which they normally exhibit more rebellion than at other times, they are still to be corrected for such wrong-doing. Proverbs 29:15 says, *"The rod and reproof give wisdom: but a child left to himself bringeth his mother to shame."* Actually, this stage of defiant disobedience is one of the first indications of a child's sin nature. Consequently, it must be dealt with when it first appears (at about the age of 12 to 18 months). If a parent fails to handle this problem initially, it will become increasingly difficult to do so. The child who begins early to win confrontations will establish a pattern of disobedience that may end in delinquency and problems in adult life.

Proverbs 29:17, *"Correct thy son, and he shall give thee rest; yea, he shall give delight unto thy soul."* Some fathers think it's cute when their little son is defiant to his mother. They respond by saying, "Wow, has he got spunk. Don't let her tell you what to do, kid. We men can't be bossed by women." Remarks like this reveal Dad's problems and are calculated to encourage disobedience. On the other hand, some mothers protect their children from Dad's strictness. "Don't spank him; he's so little." Or possibly both parents ignore defiance hoping it will go away; they don't want to mar an evening's tranquility. However, ignoring the problem only postpones the unpleasantness. The problem worsens, and the parents finally become so exasperated at the child's continued defiance that they explode in anger and punish him too severely. Handling small problems immediately will prevent bigger problems in the future.

The parental response of definite, swift, sure disciplinary action will change a child's behavior. Anger, exasperated screaming, and yelling, don't bring about change; it is the decided punishment following the angry outburst that convinces children. When our granddaughter was two-and-a-half, we were in a cafeteria; her mother brought her food on a yellow tray. She shoved it away in an outburst of temper, for she had wanted a red tray. Her mother immediately picked her up, took her out, and spanked her. When she brought her back, she settled down to eat from the yellow tray with no further problem. If her mother had tried to change the food to another tray and given in to her defiance, additional incidents at the meal would have made the time unpleasant for all of us. Mother and Dad should agree ahead of time on how they will handle such problems of defiance; they should not allow themselves to be caught off-guard.

A child readily understands corporal punishment. Proverbs 23:13-14 says, *"Withhold not correction from the child: for if thou beatest him with the rod, he shall not die. Thou shalt beat him with the rod, and shalt deliver his soul from hell."* The child should be spanked with an instrument such as a switch or a light paddle that will sting. Proverbs 22:15, *"Foolishness is bound in the heart of a child; but the rod of correction shall drive it far from him."* Spanking should also be done deliberately and without anger. The low, calm, intense "I-mean-business" voice is important. After the spanking, the parent must follow through and see that the child does what he has been told to do. It is also important that the parent communicates love, not rejection, after corporal punishment.

Though a very young child really understands only corporal punishment, older children, at three or four years of age, may also understand other forms of punishment such as isolation for 10 or 15 minutes in the corner. A good explanation should follow a spanking or any other form of correction. For the first few times, a child may try to show defiance even after a spanking. In such cases he is testing his will against his parent's authority. The parent must change the child's behavior, even if it means two or three spankings for the same offense (this may occur once or twice during the two-year-old stage). Remember Proverbs 19:18, *"Chasten thy son while there is hope, and let not thy soul spare for his crying."* The child feels secure once he realizes there are definite boundary lines.

Teaching the child to make choices. Allowing children to make choices in a matter on their age level not only trains them for later life but also eliminates some of the difficulties that arise from their desire for independence. When our children were small, they could spend a nickel a week of their allowances. They could choose anything from penny candy to nickel bars; if they wanted an ice cream bar or a big candy bar, they learned to wait a week and save until they could get what they wanted. Parents should give children as many opportunities for choices as possible, making the choice definite, i.e., "Do you want to wear the blue dress or the white one today?" "Would you like to go to the park or for a hike in the woods?"

Refusing to let mealtimes and bedtime become attention-getting or crisis times. Having very simple rules at these times prevents problems. For example, the wise parent puts a small amount of food on the child's plate, then allows him to get more if he desires to do so. The parent may make the child take a taste of everything on the table, but should not make him eat a big helping of every-

thing. Like adults, children have their own prefer-
ences, but making them taste new foods helps children learn to enjoy them.

During this two-year-old stage, children do not
necessarily grow constantly. Therefore, they don't
need the same amount of food from day to day. If a
child doesn't feel like eating at mealtime, the mother
should take his plate away, and give him only milk,
raw fruit and vegetables, or protein between meals.
Sugar snacks such as candy, jello, or cookies will dull
his appetite and cause his blood sugar level to fall
considerably. This change results in crankiness and
a rejection of good food except for the sweets he
now craves. Because children are often hungry
about an hour before supper, it may be more
pleasant for all if they could eat part of their meal
early. Withholding food or sending a child to bed
without food should never be used as a means of
punishment.

Bed-time should be a quiet, story-telling time
when children are taken—not sent off—to bed.
Going through a regular bedtime routine that they
can learn to enjoy will give them security. Both
Mother and Dad can participate in the story-telling
and devotions. If these principles are followed, the
children won't feel as if they are being exiled from
the warmth of the family circle by being sent off to
bed. A warm bath, a cup of milk, snuggling in front
of the fire, and soft music are usually soothing to
the active child.

Enjoying children in day-by-day situations.
During many daily activities and chores, parents
should play games, sing, and work with their children. Work can be a time of enjoyment and family

fellowship. Two- and three-year-olds love to help Mother with cleaning, dishes, and other easy chores. When our granddaughter was two-and-a-half, she was able to clear the table and load the dishwasher. Children must be taught to work, but work time need not be tedious. Making a game out of eating, going to bed, or doing chores takes a bit of imagination on mother's part; but it quickly eliminates the confusion and frayed nerves.

Singing little phrases and ditties which include the child's name can get him motivated for positive activities. We play a simple little song on the piano about our three-year-old granddaughter. "Tammy is a good little girl; Tammy obeys her mother. Tammy does it right away; Tammy does it with a smile."

Using imagination in difficult situations turns them into times of fun and happiness. One mother couldn't get her daughter to eat her cereal, so she made up a story about a little "growl" in her daughter's stomach who was hungry and begging to be fed. The little girl from then on, with the fun of feeding the tiny "growl," ate all kinds of things.

Giving children love and attention for their emotional survival. Given for good behavior, this attention is called positive reinforcement. The parent who gives children attention and rewards them for whining and crying is encouraging bad behavior. The more attention parents give, such as playing and working with a child when he is young, the less he will need later on in life, for the attention-need has been fulfilled. The demonstrations of love should be unconditional, despite the child's behavior, i.e., kissing, hugging, cuddling, and saying "I love you."

The typical two-year-old, experiencing his first nightmares, feels insecure and needs Mother and Dad immediately for reassurance and love. Most children will cry out, and Mother and Dad will hurry to their room to console them. The child may inquire about noises or shadows. During these times parents should pick the child up and take him to the window to see the cause of the noise, touch the shadow he has seen, shut the closet door, or merely explain what he saw or heard. Parents should take time to give necessary reassurances before leaving the child. If the child comes into the parents' bedroom, a few minutes of snuggling in Mom and Dad's bed is good reassurance. One parent should then get up and carry the child to his bed, changing or taking him to the bathroom if necessary. Children should not, however, be allowed to sleep with their parents. Permitted over a period of time this habit is difficult to break and could cause psychological problems.

A mother must be aware of her child's simultaneous feelings of attraction and repulsion toward her and conversely, her ambivalent feelings toward her child. One mother of a two-year-old called me, crying, and said, "My son hates me. He called me a bad name." While the mother was talking, I could hear him in the background saying, "I want my mommy." I explained a two-year-old's typical feelings and then suggested she go back and meet his needs. A mother would have the same mixed feelings when little Joey has wandered out of the yard and disappeared. After a frantic three-hour search, Mother finds him watching TV in a neighbor's home—the neighbor unaware of his being there. Overjoyed with relief that the boy has been found, the mother is still angry with the boy for the consternation and trouble he has caused. Having to send the police away and an angry husband back to work doesn't make it easier for a wife to sort out her feelings. We need to show positive love at these times. Punishment is in order only if the child has been disobedient or rebellious. Children should not be punished when they are unaware that their behavior has been unacceptable.

Realizing that the two-year-old age is a unique learning time. The young child learns by asking questions, investigating, handling, touching, feeling, looking, climbing, taking apart, putting together, and creating. All of these activities are a part of his learning experiences. Many mothers get very irritated by these activities and curtail them by excessively spanking the child or putting him into a playpen for long periods of time. (For short periods of time while the mother gets supper or does house work, a playpen is fine but the child ought to have verbal contact with his mother, as well as many things to see, handle, and play with in the playpen.) Mother can increase a child's learning experiences by singing alphabet ditties, encouraging the child's investigation into certain things, and explaining the who, what, when, where and why.

Turning the question back to the child also helps his thinking process and develops self-confidence. For example, if the child asks, "Why is the kitty eating his food?" The mother might reply, "Honey, why do you eat your food?" He will answer, "Because I'm hungry and the kitty is hungry." He has analyzed the situation and has come to a logical conclusion. Children should be encouraged to find answers, then introduced to the sources where they can find the answers. For example, "Let's ask your grandfather when he comes over for supper; he knows all about things like that" or "Let's look in this bird book; I think there is a picture of it in here."

Parents should be alert to the many teachable moments in daily experiences—the cat having kittens, the birds eating their food, the sunlight forming a rainbow on the wall as it passes through the glass, the tea kettle whistling, or the high wind wailing outside.

HANDLING SPECIFIC CAUSES OF DIFFICULTIES

Several things may provoke small children to exhibit unacceptable behavior such as whining, crying, pouting, contrariness, mischievousness or tormenting.

The first cause of such behavior is fatigue in either the mother or child. Children seem to have more energy than their parents. When mother gets tired, she may become inconsistent in her discipline and relinquish the control that should be maintained. She may become short-tempered, sharp, and defensive with the children. Her screaming or yelling only complicates the problem. Because it takes a rested mother to handle children, a nap when the children are resting will help solve these problems.

Children also become unruly when they are tired. They will refuse to act acceptably. When whining or crying comes on, it is often a sign that the children are hot and need a drink or that they are very tired and need a nap. Keeping cool drinks placed low enough in the refrigerator for children to reach, then making sure children drink enough liquids is one of the first steps in calming a child down. Likewise, if a mother knows that the child has lost sleep, she should make sure he has a good nap, which will make a big difference in his behavior. Children should have a rest time every afternoon. They may not go to sleep, but they at least need to unwind.

Certain foods will also cause unacceptable behavior. A theoretical common cause of children's emotional upsets is excessive sugar which irritates or stimulates the brain and may result in hyperactivity and emotional upset. Sugar-coated cereals, most of which have over 50 percent sugar, are one of the main sources of excess sugar, but eating candy and cookies given by doting grandparents and well-meaning friends can also result in misbehavior. Furthermore, an ingredient in chocolate similar to the caffeine in coffee or tea may cause irritability and restlessness in children. Cutting down on sugar and on other problem foods can prevent trouble from arising.

A third specific cause of misbehavior is boredom. On rainy or snowy days or on days when they have no one to play with and nothing to do, children become bored. Mothers sometimes become exasperated with just keeping the kids busy, but they need to devise some activities which will keep preschoolers busy at times like these. Having such supplies as a record player to play children's records, pictures to cut from a catalog, paste or play dough, paints, colorforms or sewing cards, blankets for making tents with dining room chairs can take much of the frustration out of play time. Helping mother clean or work on other projects can also keep children busy during these times. For example, cleaning sinks (children love that kind of water play), working in the garden, and dusting bookshelves are all helpful and interesting chores for children to do when they are bored.

The fourth cause of misbehavior is excessive energy. Walking, running, exercising, playing ball, chasing up and down stairs or performing gymnastics all help children to use up this energy. Supervised bathtub play or play in an outdoor pool can burn up a lot of energy. All children should have plenty of time outside. On rainy or snowy days they need to have some other place to cut loose and release this energy—a basement or playroom may be such a place, although a half-hour walk with Dad in the rain or snow burns up a lot of energy.

Handling a two-year-old can be pleasant and rewarding if these simple, common-sense principles are followed.

14 The Generation Gap

Is the generation gap getting worse, or are there common, fundamental problems in dealing with teens that have existed in all ages? Nearly 3000 years ago, the Greek poet Hesiod complained, "I see no hope for the future of our people if they are dependent on the frivolous youth of today, for certainly all youth are reckless beyond words. . . . When I was a boy, we were taught to be discreet and respectful of elders, but the present youth are exceedingly wise and impatient of restraint." Over 100 years ago, the Rev. B. Silliman Ives, in an article in the New York *Times*, described the teenagers of 1864: "For the last ten years , I have been a close observer of what has passed among the rising generation in this great metropolis, and I cannot suppress the humiliating conviction that even pagan Rome in the corrupt age of Augustus never witnessed among certain classes of the young a more utter disregard of honor, truth, and piety, and even the common decencies of life!" Hal Boyle, a popular newspaper columnist, in 1951 described the adolescent boy as "dressing like a bum and having the manners of an ape." It seems that there has always been this plight called the "generation gap."

Youth workers, parents, and teachers need to understand some of the causes and the steps to take to bridge this chasm. Some feel that the only way to reach a teenager is to be like him in dress and life-style. This is folly and defeat, for teenagers are looking for mature adults to guide them in the way they should go. Teens want to be understood, not mimicked. Parents who are willing to take the time and to show the proper interest can close the "gap." This generation gap exists because of faults on the part of both parents and teenagers. Impatient, insecure, indifferent, and inconsistent parents seem to be crucial factors in producing this lack of understanding.

Parental impatience is evident in most families because parents forget that teenagers, though they appear to be adults, are still learning a great number of things. Teenagers seemingly "are always making stupid mistakes and doing dumb things" because they do not have the knowledge or experience needed for various situations. Susie, cooking the evening meal in Mother's kitchen and leaving out some essential ingredient, is not helped by Mother's impatience and ridicule. Dad, under the car asking for a three-quarter-inch socket wrench and getting instead a pipe wrench, may burst into an undeserved tirade against his youngster—especially if the father bumps his head on the fender while climbing out to get the right tool.

Insecurity in parents who are faced with urgent, monumental questions causes many misunderstandings. The 15-year-old girl who asks if she can go to the beach for the weekend with six other girls during Easter vacation or the boy who asks if he can use his $200 savings as a down payment on a snow-mobile is presenting unforeseen questions demanding unrehearsed decisions. The parents can eliminate a lot of difficulty here by refusing to give instant decisions. They can rather wait until they get all the facts, discuss them with the children and other participants, weigh the pros and cons of the situation, and then promise the teenager an answer at a future, specified time. Further discussions with the teenager before rendering a final decision may be in order also. But the parents must agree and present a unified front on any decision. The youngster should never be allowed to use a problem to drive a wedge between the mother and father or to start a family fight. Many times the parents may have to point out to the teenager the folly or impracticality of his plan; in this case, good facts and figures can aid the discussion. In this way, parents are actually teaching some good methods and steps in problem-solving. The father, of course, should always have the veto power over any decision and should have the right and responsibility to make certain these decisions are made in line with the goals of the family.

A third thing that turns teenagers from their parents is indifference. Parents tend to get very busy and involved with their own important activities and look upon teenagers' activities as being frivolous. A daughter's being elected cheerleader or a son's being appointed manager of the football team is very important, and teenagers want to talk these things over with their parents, who need to take the time to find out what their children are doing, what is going on at school, and how they feel about these things. By the same token, however, parents need to be careful about appearing to pry into or control their teenagers' activities. Communicating is helpful in avoiding this misconception.

Parental inconsistency is another detriment in the relationship between parents and teens. Teenagers are well able to discern when parents are motivated by profit instead of principle. They are willing to listen to adult prohibitions and admonitions if they can see the adults consistently living these principles in their own lives. When a teenage son knows that Dad is the messiest person in the whole family and keeps Mother busy full-time picking up after him, he is unlikely to listen to his father's admonition to keep his room neat. It is hard to admit, but children usually are a reflection of their parents' own character and habits. Many teenagers have been turned against God because of the hypocrisy of their deacon father or Sunday-school-teacher mother. Teens desperately need Spirit-filled parents who lead consistent lives and have consistent testimonies.

Teenagers with their desire for independence, their instant idealism, and their immaturity share the blame for the generation gap, although adults must realize that the teenager is the learner and the adult is the teacher. Teens have a natural desire for independence and are usually trying to get out from under authority to gain their freedom of choice and action. Every teenager must fully comprehend the admonition in Ephesians 6:1-3 that children are to obey their parents. Teenagers are considered children as long as they are financially and emotionally dependent on their parents. Of course, parents must take definite steps in helping them to gain proper independence so that they can function maturely as adults when they cease to be teenagers.

Teenagers need counseling concerning marriage and vocational decisions without Dad or Mother making their decisions for them. A lifetime of working at a job or living through a marriage that was chosen by another is the worst kind of cancerous misery.

Parents can make broad vocational suggestions early in the child's life—suggestions in line with his natural abilities, interests, and talents. Very early, when the child is in junior high, the parents should try to assess the intelligence, abilities, and talents of their child and make these results known to the teenager so he can make valid decisions.

Most above-average children should plan on college; C grades or above are the best predictors for success in college. College plans should include a Christian college large enough to allow for a wide range of choices. A recent survey of college seniors revealed that 50 percent had changed their major at least once since entering as a freshman. Especially when the child is on the college level, the parents should have little or nothing to do with such a decision other than to counsel and give pertinent information related to the matter. However, parents can press strongly the benefits of full-time Christian service and pray regarding a dedicated life of this kind of service for their child.

This same attitude should prevail in the choice of a marriage partner. Parents can establish wise guidelines in line with II Corinthians 6:14-18; that is, the teenagers should not date unsaved or divorced people, and they should be encouraged to date people from a good home background and heritage. Parents should, of course, set the limits on dating concerning the time the child should begin to date, the minimum age when he is permitted to go steady, and the type of chaperoning (double date, etc.). Dating in junior high, except to group functions, and going steady in high school can lead to some real problems. Guidelines for engagement and marriage should include what we may call the three "F's": 1) Finish school, whether it be college, technical, or nursing school.   2) Financial preparedness. Teenagers ought to be financially responsible, that is, prepared to pay the numerous bills that come during engagement and the first few years of marriage such as the engagement ring, honeymoon, setting up housekeeping (rent, furniture, transportation, utilities, apartment deposit, etc.).   3) Family responsibilities. Every couple getting married should be prepared for a baby within the first several years, for they can never be certain that pregnancy will not occur.

Teenagers learn to make decisions by making a number of successful choices along life's pathway. They will also learn by their mistakes. A good counseling rapport with a child, starting early in his life, will develop into the right kind of relationship after the child becomes an adult. Parents should have so trained their child that by the time he reaches the age of 20, the parents have become friends rather than controllers. The parents' goal should be to train their children to become independent.

Besides wanting independence, teenagers also tend to be idealistic, and the teen period is characterized by instant idealism. They want to cure society by solving its problems today or burning it down tomorrow. They are action-oriented individuals, and they find it hard to accept the fact that social evils and problems cannot be solved immediately. They have been conditioned by seeing complex problems solved within an hour on some television program or by assurances from the news media that a politician with a massive amount of government money can take care of anything. The social and political processes of adult society are time-consuming and frustrating even to adults, and teenagers have to learn to work within the framework of society rather than trying to kick it apart. Radical groups play upon teenagers' instant idealism by trying to divert this energy into channels serving their own ends and diabolical purposes.

Many teens have rejected the traditional goals and values of their parents as being materialistic and unworthy of their devotion and energy and too restrictive upon their feeling-oriented lifestyle. This rejection leads not only to an attitude of futility and hopelessness because they are convinced there are no real "successes" in life, but also to a lowered self-concept, and even a sense of worthlessness. They then become confused about their role and identity. Adults can encourage teens to set worthwhile life goals based upon God's purposes for their life and help them to achieve short-range goals that bring a feeling of success and achievement, which is vitally important to a good self-concept.

Teenagers are also marked by immaturity. They have never been down this road before; they have never thought through certain problems; they have never lived through certain situations. Good discussions at the dinner table on problems and issues of the day help the teenager to sharpen his own planning and goal setting, putting his activities into proper perspective. Discussing family problems with the teenager and seeing the eventual results work out as a consequence of the family's praying, good planning, working, and waiting bring confidence and develop the teen's own leadership abilities. Mature Christian parents learn not to overreact to the teenagers' wild schemes, ideas, or feelings. A calm, Spirit-filled reaction showing understanding by listening, discernment by questioning, and guidance by directing them to biblical principles—these will keep things calm when some other reaction may touch off a family uproar.

The fundamental difference between the mature adult generation and the teenage generation is the teenager's need of learning to control his fleshly and sensual nature with its many surges and urges, and of conquering the immature tendency to operate on feelings rather than on basic standards and values. Parents must teach their teenagers to control their feelings and apply good, basic principles to everyday situations. Actions and reactions should be based on predetermined values, not on the feeling of the moment. Good feelings follow right action. The mature person learns to do what is right and to do right at the appropriate time, whether he feels like it or not. It takes youth a while to learn this lesson. They need guidance from mature adults in learning how to "cope rather than elope" with the world, the flesh, and the devil.

Mature parents, teachers, and youth leaders can

do a great deal to lessen the generation gap and create understanding. They must take the responsibility for the adults that come out of their homes, classrooms, and youth groups.

15   Building Character in the Home

Because of a lack of knowledge about character and how it is developed, building character in a child is probably the most difficult and most neglected task of a parent.

Character may be defined as living and acting according to a pre-determined set of life principles. A person with character does not act by impulse and is not subject to peer pressure. He does not base his decisions on feeling. An example—Boy Scouts are said to have character when they live and act in accordance with the 12 Scout laws and their motto of "Be prepared."

A Christian acquires a life direction, particular stamp, mold or impress at salvation—this is the start of Christian character. In Matthew 7:26 Jesus said, *"Every one that heareth these sayings of mine, and doeth them not, shall be likened unto a foolish man, which built his house upon the sand."* One who tries to build character without Christ builds on a shaky foundation. However, true character develops when a person learns to act and live according to biblical principles. These biblical truths may be referred to as Bible Action

Truths, (see Appendix for a full explanation of these), BAT's.

People without character tend to be feeling-oriented; they act on their feelings rather than on principle. This generation tends to encourage this type of behavior because of three cultural innovations that have become prominent in the last 20 to 30 years.

The first of these innovations is television. TV is not a mind-oriented media; it is feeling-oriented. A person doesn't really think through a television program; he "feels" through it. Children are usually subject to 24 hours weekly of this passive reception. They have no active participation in their TV watching; consequently, they are influenced both mentally and physically toward a feeling-oriented view of life. The prevalent idea of "do your own thing" is an off-shoot of this philosophy.

A second cultural influence is rock music. It's not a mind-oriented music at all; it is sensual, feeling-oriented. The louder and more repetitive it becomes, the more it influences the listener's sensual feelings. The lyrics to most rock songs condition children to concentrate on the sensual, feeling-oriented life style of drugs and sex.

A third of these cultural developments is found in the popular humanistic philosophy. This philosophy has been steadily increasing in influence over the last 30 years; it permeates the teaching and curriculum of the government schools on all levels—elementary, secondary, and college alike. The teachers, textbooks, and overall environment of today's public education system fosters this humanistic climate, which is drastically affecting the behavior and thinking of young people.

If parents are going to teach Christian character, they must first of all minimize these influences by cutting the TV watching in their homes to a bare minimum, by eliminating all rock music (including so-called gospel rock), and by getting their children into Christian schools that will train them to live by biblical principles and thus aid in Christian character development. A character-building Christian school must have dedicated, qualified teachers; sound Christian textbooks, and a disciplined social environment that will produce standards conducive to building good character.

Along with eliminating negative influences and placing their children in a Christian school environment, the parents must also institute a positive program of character education in the home. The first step in this program is to establish a set of biblical principles that contain the various elements of character that young people need to develop. A set of such principles has been developed by the Bob Jones University School of Education. Entitled "Teaching Bible Action Truths," it is published in chart form by the School of Education (see Appendix B). These 37 Bible Action Truths are conveniently grouped under eight action and reaction categories, and a handy 4-M formula for grasping these truths accompanies the chart. The 4-M Formula is based on the principles found in Psalm 119:9, 11, 15, and 17 and contains four basic elements for learning these Bible Action Truths.

A second step in character training in the home is providing stories, children's books, and readers that help the child to get involved vicariously in sit-

uations in which the characters are applying principles in their lives. Good examples of this type of
story are the old McGuffey readers and Aesop's
Fables. Stories such as these are character-building
stories. Although they are not always Christian
stories, they do teach principles and encourage
children to act in accordance with principle.

A third way of teaching character is to use
slogans that will remind the child of principles being
taught. Some good examples are "Finish the job";
"Do right"; "Quitters never win"; "Make up your
mind"; and "Keep on keeping on." Most people have
a backlog of slogans they were taught as children
and can use these same slogans in training their
own children. Such slogans can help children in
critical situations the same way that they have
helped parents at various times in their lives.

A fourth aspect of character building is the
positive example of parents, teachers, and youth
workers who are consistently living according to
biblical principles. One of the main causes of youth
conflicts is a lack of consistency in the home:
mothers and dads who are not providing the character examples that their children need to see daily.
Such parents who refuse to follow biblical principles
consistently in their own lives will have daily problems—problems that will be detrimental to their
children. The child's learning in Sunday school
classes, Bible classes, and Christian school classes
will be hindered by the primary place of learning—
the home.

A fifth method of positive teaching would be
action projects that can be carried out in the home,
Christian school, or youth group. For example, in

the home, a regular work project such as a paper route can be an effective character building influence. Such a project can help the child learn to be punctual and financially responsible, as well as reliable despite weather conditions or other uncomfortable circumstances.

Christian schools need to provide opportunity for student participation and leadership training through various school projects, programs, junior/senior high banquets, trips, and weekend or camp retreats. Through these activities, young people can apply the Bible action truths they are learning in their homes and their schools.

Through their youth groups, teenagers can help out in various church activities: televangelism, counseling, neighborhood Bible clubs, vacation Bible school, Sunday school, or any other of numerous projects that demand high-level responsibility, initiative, and reliability. The old adage of "use me or lose me" should challenge youth pastors to carry out some of these projects. Children learn to take responsibility as they are given tasks and made to meet deadlines and to accept success or failure in their ventures.

A sixth, and probably most important aspect in character training is accountability: a child's awareness that he is accountable to God (Romans 14:12), and then to others, for what he should do. Parents need to supervise and check to see that tasks are completed and responsibilities discharged.

Character building must be a deliberate effort and not left to chance. Fathers and mothers have probably the greatest influence upon a child's character. One expert suggests a life notebook in which the children keep a record of the various lessons and experiences that God has used to develop their character.

Parents who truly believe that the Bible contains the life principles for proper living, Christlikeness, and an abundant life are going to develop a program for training their children in these principles. In the past, parents and teachers may have emphasized biblical facts rather than principles; but facts are too easily forgotten, whereas the Bible principles can become part of daily living. Facts may be the medium, but they are not the message. While teaching these principles, parents must help their children to be constantly aware of their personal contact with Jesus Christ as Saviour and Lord of their lives. Young people can very easily get their eyes on principles and miss Jesus Christ, who is the purpose and motivation of character.

Personal discipline is a vital part of good Christian character, for humans are naturally feeling-directed and impulse-oriented. Materialism, moral looseness, and self-indulgent living can cause even Christians to reject the idea of control, restraint, or self-denial. Yet personal discipline is essential in developing character and in training children to follow one's example.

Personal discipline involves being organized, consistent, and purposeful. This goal is accomplished by bringing one's feelings and actions under the control of a Spirit-filled mind. A disciplined Christian, therefore, is one who:

Consistently carries out responsibilities and goes beyond the call of duty (Matthew 25:21).

Sets goals and reaches these goals with planned

efficiency (Philippians 3:13; Proverbs 13:12, 19).

Is governed by a sense of love and responsibility to others (John 13:34, 35).

Looks upon life's problems as challenges that need dynamic solutions and knows that God has allowed these problems for his good (Romans 8:28; I Thessalonians 5:18).

Submits to authority and imposed rules and regulations with a cooperative spirit (I Timothy 6:1-8; Romans 13:1-5).

Personal discipline is the determination to let God, rather than your feelings, control your life. For Paul said in I Corinthians 6:12, *"All things are lawful unto me, but all things are not expedient: all things are lawful for me, but I will not be brought under the power of any."* As Richard Taylor stated in his book *The Disciplined Life,* "Disciplined character belongs to the person who achieves balance by bringing all his faculties and powers under control." Discipline is not getting a rigid set of rules and slavishly denying normal desires and bodily pleasures, for Colossians 2:20-23 says, *"Wherefore if ye be dead with Christ from the rudiments of the world, why, as though living in the world, are ye subject to ordinances, (Touch not; taste not; handle not; Which all are to perish with the using;) After the commandments and doctrines of men? Which things have indeed a shew of wisdom in will worship, and humility, and neglecting of the body; not in any honour to the satisfying of the flesh."* Christians who are under grace and who put themselves back under law again begin to have serious difficulties in their lives.

Personal discipline is achieved when a Christian makes up his mind to let the Holy Spirit control all areas of his life.

A Spirit-controlled thought life. What a person thinks is vitally important. Thoughts control decisions, decisions control behavior, behavior controls feelings. Corrupt behavior and guilt feelings follow uncontrolled fantasizing. While no one knows another's innermost thoughts, they eventually are revealed in one way or another. Proverbs 4:23 tells us to *"Keep thy heart with all diligence; for out of it are the issues of life."* Matthew 12:34, 35 also states, *"For out of the abundance of the heart the mouth speaketh. A good man out of the good treasure of the heart bringeth forth good things: and an evil man out of the evil treasure bringeth forth evil things."* God wants the Christian to rid himself of negative, devilish thoughts. II Corinthians 10:5 says *"Casting down imaginations, and every high thing that exalteth itself against the knowledge of God, and bringing into captivity every thought to the obedience of Christ."* He would have us to think positive faith thoughts continually (Philippians 4:8).

Spirit-controlled emotions. Anger and fear are usually harmful emotions and need to be harnessed and brought under the Holy Spirit's control. How does a Christian act and react toward others when they have been threatening or abusive? Does a Christian allow other people's behavior to govern his behavior; does he allow others' problems to become his problems by a wrong emotional response? Or does he let the Holy Spirit control his emotional response? Emotions can enrich a life if they are allowed to develop within God's control and guidelines. Proverbs 16:32 states, *"He that is slow to anger is better than the mighty; and he that ruleth his spirit than he that taketh a city."* Proverbs 25:28 conversely states, *"He that hath no rule over his own spirit is like a city* *that is broken down, and without walls."* Proverbs 29:22, *"An angry man stirreth up strife, and a furious man aboundeth in transgression."* II Timothy 1:7, *"For God hath not given us the spirit of fear; but of power, and of love, and of a sound mind."* Strong faith and trust in a mighty God erases fearful, neurotic, worried behavior (Philippians 4:6-7). Emotions and moods must be governed correctly if the Christian is to have disciplined character.

Spirit-controlled bodily desires and appetites. Many people pamper their bodies to such an extent that any lack of "creature comforts" becomes intolerable and burdensome; for example, having to live as many missionaries do would be more than some could abide. But where is the ruggedness of the pioneer spirit, the spirit of those who reached their goals despite hardships? Nowadays the overriding goal seems to be having "munchies" and a cold soft drink in one hand and operating the TV by remote control with the other.

Along this same line, appetite and sex desire can be a blessing and a pleasure when controlled and practiced according to God's principles. I Corinthians 9:25-27 says, *"And every man that striveth for the mastery is temperate in all things. Now they do it to obtain a corruptible crown; but we an incorruptible. I therefore so run, not as uncertainly; so fight I, not as one that beateth the air: But I keep under my body, and bring it into subjection: lest that by any means, when I have preached to others, I myself should be a castaway."* Galatians 5:24 also instructs us, *"And they that are Christ's have crucified the flesh with the affections and lusts."* I Thessalonians 4:4, *"That every one of you should know how to possess his vessel in sanctification and honour."* God can bless the Christian who willingly decides to use his body, with its desires and appetites, to His glory (I Corinthians 10:31).

Spirit-controlled conversation. The tongue, above all things, needs to be controlled. Ephesians 4:29 indicates that the Christian is to let no corrupt communication come out of his mouth. Instead, he should use his speech to edify and help. As an old Scotsman said, "I taste my words 'ere they pass my teeth." James 3:1-13 compares the tongue to a bit in a horse's mouth; both are small things that can take complete control. It also compares the tongue to a rudder on a ship and indicates that the tongue is able to direct the whole body. Verse 13 concludes that a man shows out of a good conversation his good works. Proverbs 29:11 reminds us, *"A fool uttereth all his mind: but a wise man keepeth it in till afterwards."* Controlling the tongue is the secret of a disciplined character.

The only way such control can be achieved is for the Christian to be filled with the Spirit of God, the Holy Spirit. Daily, he must determine to deny the flesh and self. Luke 9:23 says, *"If any man will come after me, let him deny himself, and take up his cross daily, and follow me."* A Christian will have disciplined character as he accepts the Holy Spirit's direction in putting God's principles into action in his daily living. Thus he may be continually conformed to the image of Jesus Christ.

"A child left to himself bringeth his mother to shame" *(Proverbs 19:15).* Character education cannot be a chance affair. In cooperation with the church and school, Christian parents must practice a planned program that will help children develop disciplined Christian character to see them through life.

16 Depression: Its Causes and Cures

Depression is becoming one of the major problems of our modern society. If it hasn't already, it probably will affect everyone's marriage and family life. According to the National Institute of Mental Health, 15 percent of the United States' adults aged 18-74 (20 million people) suffer from significant depressive illnesses each year. Approximately one-third of all adult women have considered suicide and about one out of every ten persons at some time needs psychological help.

Pastors and Christian counselors also agree that depression frequently saps the spiritual strength of God's people. One man wrote, "How do you fight off depression when you are uncertain what the cause is? I ask this because I have a vague heavy feeling and can't seem to be able to get excited about things which are important. I feel wretched and alone most of the time and feel that no one really cares whether I live or die. I used to have a zeal for the things of God, but lately I seem to have lost the power I once had in prayer and witnessing. My appetite is gone; I wake up early in the morning, yet

I'm always tired. I doubt my salvation and sometimes wonder if I've committed the unpardonable sin. Can you help?"

There is help. The causes of depression are both physical and psychological. However, before a cure can be prescribed the cause must be determined.

PHYSICAL CAUSES

Cycles: One physical reason for depression is periodic changes in the body. Humans tend to be on basic cycles. Women are particularly affected by hormone cycles. They usually experience three to four up and down (depressed) cycles monthly. Men may also notice such an up and down cycle, but they usually have only one low point every 30 to 40 days. Plotting depression times and anticipating the low points enables one to take preventative action. Scheduling activities and social events, and setting goals to accomplish during these low times can help keep a person from slipping into despondency.

Anemia: Another physical factor is anemia, a lack of iron. Again, women are more susceptible than men. Two symptoms of anemia are fuzzy thinking and depression. A simple blood test during a regular check-up can determine if a person needs additional iron. Good nutrition and vitamins (plus iron) will help.

Low Blood Sugar: A low blood sugar level (hypoglycemia) is often caused by poor eating habits. The solution—eat a balanced diet with adequate protein and fewer sugar or carbohydrate foods. Munching nuts or cheese between meals, drinking milk for snacks, and eating a well-balanced breakfast are all important factors. It is best also not to allow four or five hours to pass before eating. Many find that a late midnight snack of protein is helpful in preventing morning depression.

Post Childbirth: The time period following childbirth may also cause depression (this period is also referred to as "post-partum blues"). Advocates of natural childbirth (LaMaze method) and breast feeding suggest that those who use these techniques are less susceptible to this type of depression. Helen Wessel, in her book *The Joy of Natural Childbirth*, points out that an understanding, supportive husband will help with the new responsibilities and, thus, alleviate much of the wife's feelings of despondency.

Hormone Upset: For some women there is a link between menopause and depression. When a woman susceptible to depression reaches the menopause, the problem may be aggravated. To stabilize this upset hormone level, some doctors recommend estrogen therapy. A pap smear can determine whether estrogen therapy is necessary. Though all doctors do not agree concerning the advisability of this type of therapy, it does seem to help in some cases. Other endocrine problems, such as thyroid, may also masquerade as depression. These problems require a doctor's diagnosis and treatment. Recent studies indicate that regular jogging, by raising the level of the catecholamines hormone in the blood, seems to relieve depression. In one study depressed patients who jogged 30 minutes three times a week significantly improved.

Fatigue: Both men and women often find that fatigue causes depression, and depression in turn causes fatigue. A recent survey of Christian married women recorded that a major cause of their depression problems and marital difficulties was fatigue.

On the average, women, especially mothers with preschoolers, need approximately one more hour of sleep than men do. Failure to get needed rest will cause these mothers to be depressed. Couples ought to consider these helpful suggestions: 1) hiring a babysitter (while the mother rests) or someone to help with the housework, 2) taking extra Vitamin B 3) starting a regular fitness program (such as jogging).

The husband should not only insist that his wife get the proper rest, but he should also help in some of the home duties to relieve some of the never-ending pressure a wife may feel. Couples should also choose their outside activities wisely; for instance, when the outside activity becomes more tiring than relaxing, it should be curtailed.

Causes of fatigue among men are overweight, aging, and a general lack of physical fitness. A well-balanced diet and a good fitness program will help do away with these common causes of male depression.

PSYCHOLOGICAL CAUSES

Guilt: The greatest cause of depression for Christians is a sense of guilt—guilt feelings arising either from past sins or present sin habits. God's Word supplies the practical, realistic solution to this problem. He assures us in I Corinthians 10:13, *"There hath no temptation taken you but such as is common to man: but God is faithful, who will not suffer you to be tempted above that ye are able; but will with the temptation also make a way to escape, that ye may be able to bear it."*

A past unconfessed sin will cause a "sin-boil" in the life. The Lord says in Isaiah 1:18 to acknowledge responsibility for sin and to confess it. Then the Christian will be freed from guilt; Christ will cleanse him (I John 1:7; Ephesians 1:7).

However, once the Christian has heeded this admonition, the Devil may cause him to doubt the forgiveness, and even his salvation. Satan would delight to have a Christian review the details of past sins, encouraging him to reason that God's goodness will prohibit His forgiveness of evil. But again, God assures Christians that once sin is confessed He will put it from Him *"as far as the east is from the west"* (Psalm 103:12) and a Christian should do the same (Philippians 3:13; Isaiah 43:18, 19, 25).

A present sin habit may also cause depression. In this case many have used the following four step formula: first, admitting the problem is a sin and confessing it; second, setting a goal for conquering the problem (for example, deciding for three days to refrain from a particular sin habit, then concentrating on reaching that goal—if there's failure, then there should be confession, setting a new goal, and beginning again); third, when tempted with a recurring sin problem, rechannelling energies into physical exercise or another activity; fourth, meditating on a verse of Scripture. This formula has helped many overcome such sin habits as smoking, overeating, drinking, and various sexual sins.

Bitterness and hatred: Another common psychological cause of depression is bitterness or hatred, especially if the hatred is directed toward some love object (mother, father, spouse, or God). When people blame God for tragic events in life, such bitterness is extremely harmful. One solution to the problem is reading I John daily for 30 days, underlining important verses which define love, and describe its influences in the life. The Word of God will have a powerful effect in changing sinful attitudes.

When dealing with sinful attitudes toward others, there are several ways to make amends: first, asking forgiveness; second, taking definite actions toward correcting the relationship—for example, a loving letter, a phone call, or an act of kindness will completely break the pattern of hate.

Negative thinking: Negative thinking has a poor effect on both the mind and body. To break its pattern, Christians must creatively rechannel their activity. For example, one woman, bored with dishwashing, pinned Bible verses on the curtains above her kitchen sink and used dishwashing time as a time for memorizing Bible verses. She creatively rechanneled her mental activity and alleviated her depression brought on by a repetitious task.

Self Pity: Self pity is another damaging attitude. Comparing oneself to others often leads to depression and thwarts the attitude of praise that every Christian should possess. Thoughts which hinder praise are described in II Corinthians 10:5 as wicked "imaginations...against God." They should be cast out of the mind and replaced with Spirit-controlled thinking. The writer of Philippians gives the positive admonition to think on things which are *"true,... honest,... just,... pure,... lovely,... and of good report" (Philippians 4:8).* Depressed Christians must replace their daily "pity party" with a definite time for praise and thankfulness.

Upsetting life events: Dr. T. H. Holmes listed in a study the top six events which cause depression. They were death of a spouse, divorce, marital separation, jail terms, death of a close relative, and personal illness or injury. These circumstances cause a dramatic change in life style and usually result in depression.

Hard work and helping others are two positive steps toward combating depression at times of emotional crisis. It is important to note, however, that extra steps must be taken for strengthening family unity when the family is fractured by one of the above upsetting events.

Some suggestions for concentrating on others at times of depressive life events are fixing a meal for another, making repairs on an elderly couple's home, or doing yard work for someone who is unable to do it himself. Doing this kind of favor will help occupy a person's thoughts with others rather than with his own unfortunate circumstances.

Christians must maintain a positive, Spirit-controlled attitude about self, situations, disappointments, and events. In everything they are to give thanks (I Thessalonians 5:18). Christ assures that *"All things work together for good to them that love God, to them who are the called according to his purpose" (Romans 8:28).*

Lack of Goals: Another lesser-known psychological cause of depression is a lack of definite goals. Many people find that setting and accomplishing goals gives great satisfaction. The Scripture states, *"Hope deferred maketh the heart sick: but when the desire cometh, it is a tree of life. The desire accomplished is sweet to the soul: but it is an abomination to fools to depart from evil"*

(Proverbs 13:12, 19).

There is, however, a caution here also: not to become enslaved to goals. Goals are a means to an end, not an end in themselves. At the end of each day, a person should check off the accomplished goals and place the unaccomplished tasks onto the next day's list, praising God for His help already evidenced and asking His strength for those tasks yet ahead (Proverbs 16:9).

Success Letdown: Success is usually followed by a letdown. Elijah provides us with a vivid example of this principle. Following his triumph on Mount Carmel, he was discouraged. He fled to the wilderness and sat under a juniper tree to talk with God. His conversation this time, however, was of a different tone—not a prayer of power, but a prayer filled with despair. *"It is enough; now, O Lord, take away my life; for I am not better than my fathers"* (I Kings 19:4).

God's servants often fall into this temptation of discouragement. Pastors' wives frequently testify that their husband's feelings of despondency follow a particularly successful Sunday. It helps, however, to realize that this natural letdown is the body's way of readjusting to normal status. During times of excitement or emergency there is a greater output of adrenalin in the circulatory system. Following these times, when the body must return to its normal state, depression often results; and the greater the success, the bigger the letdown.

Color and Music: Many people may be unaware of the effects of color and music on their moods. For example, dull, dark colors in the home sometimes have a depressive effect; likewise, primary colors may uplift the spirits. Thus, bright colors in the kitchen, especially yellow, usually have a positive effect on women.

Music can also affect moods. Plaintive, nostalgic pieces may have a depressive effect, particularly if they are associated with some unpleasant memories. Other types of music may calm or lighten spirits. Scripture again gives us an example: Saul called for David to play his harp when Saul was troubled by an evil spirit (I Samuel 16:14-23). A depressed person might listen to marches or hymns of rejoicing and praise to help overcome his negative mood.

For frequent periods of depression, a person should first see a physician for a complete physical check-up. No amount of counseling will help a person suffering from a severe physical difficulty. Describing the depressed periods to the doctor— noting the times of day, the events, and situations— will give him clues as to the cause of the problem.

If the cause is not physical, then a Christian should call upon the Lord to aid him in the problem, freely talking it over with Him and a spouse also (a pastor, too, if necessary). God desires that Christians be happy (John 10:10b). Anyone who is not enjoying the blessings of life should begin to look for the cause and make up his mind to apply the necessary steps to cure depression.

17 Successful Family Finances

High prices, inflation, and having too much month left over at the end of the money seem to be common plights. Having to eke out an existence for shelter, food, and clothing, however, doesn't seem to be today's crucial problem. The real problem Americans face is desiring bigger and better, keeping up with their social peers, or getting the good life they think they deserve (Proverbs 27:20). Having faith in money matters, as well as in all areas of life, is important for a happy family life. Certain principles, if followed, can bring finances into line and help to turn this area of defeat into a victory.

Principle 1: Having the Bible attitude about money. Matthew 6 gives some good teaching on money. Verse 3 indicates that Christians are not to flaunt their money, especially in their giving, but rather to use what they have discreetly as unto the Lord. Verses 19-21 say not to lay up treasures here on earth where they will be corrupted, but rather lay up treasures in heaven. *"For where your treasure is, there will your heart be also."* Verses 25-33 caution against worrying about finances, rather than being content with food and raiment, for God will always provide for His own. Yes, this is living a hand-to-mouth existence, but it is God's hand to His children's mouths. Verses 33-34 also tell us that our true goal should be God and His righteousness, not material gain. Verse 24 also warns us that money can become a god; Christians need, therefore, to decide which god they are going to serve. I Timothy 6:6-10 stresses the idea of contentment with godliness, indicating in verse 10 that the love of money is the root of all evil, and a person will pierce himself through with many sorrows if he loves money.

A man, in particular, must be concerned about providing for his household; for if he fails to do so, he is considered to be worse than an infidel (I Timothy 5:8). Husbands would do well then to follow the principles in Proverbs 3:9-10 regarding their income. If they will consistently give of the first fruits or the first tenth of all their increase (including wages, things given to them, things produced by their labor, i.e., a garden), God will prosper them and keep their barns full and their presses bursting out with new wine. A good sign that a person has the right attitude toward money is his willingness to take at least ten percent of his income and immediately give it to the Lord. He can give offerings above this ten percent and also give to the poor, but the first tenth should always go immediately to God if a person wants His blessing and material prosperity.

The devil will use the love of money to capture the hearts and minds of people. Christians should resist the daily advertising bombardment of TV, newspapers, and magazines, which often create a

spirit of discontent and produce a materialistic attitude. A Christian must maintain God's view of
money if he desires a contented married life.

**Principle 2: Budgeting and planning family fi-
nances.** Couples should have both a plan for saving
and a plan for investing. The Christian family will,
as stated, take the first tenth of their income and
give it to the Lord, and they will then take the
second tenth of their income to use for investing to
earn additional money. These investments include
real estate or equipment that will increase the
money invested. Too many people save to spend
instead of saving to invest. Couples could then use
the other 80 percent of the income for their needs—
food, shelter, clothing, utilities, taxes, and other
essentials that must be a part of a good budget.

Listed below is a simple outline of a typical budget with minimum percentages.

10%	Church giving
10%	Savings
25%	Home
	(rent, mortgage, furnishings, repairs)
30%	Food
15%	Taxes
5%	Transportation
5%	Incidentals
	(insurance, cleaning)

Couples should do this planning before spending
the paycheck. Both husband and wife should cooperate in making up the budget of all their income
and then keeping that budget. Most husbands feel

reluctant to spend money, for they are always under the responsibility to provide for the future needs of the family; thus, they should make the final decisions concerning big expenditures. Impulsive buying and charge accounts place people under financial pressure and are the cause of many upsets in the marriage relationship. Instead, extra money received as gifts for Christmas, birthdays, etc., may be spent for the special items that the wife desires such as a dishwasher, microwave, or mixer. Couples also need a regular time to plan and revise the budget during the year. A good budget mixed with faith in God to supply needs will solve many problems and save much worry.

Principle 3: Saving money. A penny saved is much more than the penny earned. The difference between "the penny saved" and "the penny earned" is that you don't have to pay income tax, social security, or unemployment taxes, on the penny saved. Therefore, a penny saved is worth about 1.45 cents.

This saving is probably most effective in grocery shopping. For example, special sales; quantity buying; seasonal, selective buying; gardening; canning; shopping at a farmer's market; or picking vegetables and fruit at a nearby farm or orchard are means to save money. Shoppers can also save by collecting, sorting, and using coupons; by buying only planned items; not giving way to impulses to stock up on junk food specials; and eliminating cookies, sugared cereals, pop, chips, and other items that will run up the grocery bill. Another idea is to use powdered milk mixed with regular milk. A family will be able to cut their grocery bill down by one-third if they will follow the above steps, remembering that a bargain is not a bargain if a family doesn't need it.

Another method of saving or economizing is for the family to make birthday and Christmas presents. Use Dad's wood-working skills and Mother's craft or cooking abilities. Making Valentine and Christmas cards and decorations can be another means of cutting costs and can be creative family fun.

In buying clothes and big-expense items, shoppers should watch for the after-holiday and mid-summer sales, being careful, however, to check the real cost of these items; for many times the item may appear on sale, but in reality the price has not been cut. Wise shoppers check equivalent prices with quantity and quality before buying large items; the consumer guide in the local library has information concerning quality and durability.

Another means of saving money is to incorporate the "Do it yourself" philosophy into the home. For example, buying a hair cutting set can eliminate the high price of hair cuts for the boys of the family. By starting when the children are young enough, a parent can become a proficient barber by the time his children are in elementary school, where it matters more how their hair looks. Getting good do-it-yourself books and learning how to do plumbing, carpentry, painting, etc., saves a good deal of money on home repair and other projects.

Principle 4: Not borrowing money on depreciating items. The Bible says in Romans 13:8, *"Owe no man any thing."* Christians should not borrow money to buy things unless the items are appreciating items. A car, boat, trailer, or stereo are depreciating items that should be paid for with cash. Couples can salvage their budget by purchasing a used car and used furniture. Also yard sales or used items advertised in newspapers or at local trading posts provide excellent bargains. Furniture depreciates in price 50 percent the first year; a car depreciates 25 percent after the first year and 15 percent the following year (totalling 40 percent after two years). Consequently, a person who is buying a used car or used furniture is actually saving a great deal of money.

Charge accounts, used only for convenience's sake or for bookkeeping purposes can be helpful; but they are unwise for small items or groceries. The average charge account increases a family's cost of living 18 percent on the unpaid balance. Time payments and finance charges can also run interest rates up as high as 18 to 48 percent. Dividing 72 by the percentage of the interest payments shows how many years of paying interest it takes to double the price of what a person is presently buying.

Principle 5: Keeping ten percent of the money invested. The rule of thumb here is to use O.P.M., other people's money in borrowing as, for example, with a mortgage on a home. Matthew 25:14-30 indicates that the faithful servant invested his talents and received a good return. Real estate is probably the best investment, and wise investors always are paying on a mortgage, since a mortgage is usually about 80 percent O.P.M. Consequently, they are making money on other people's money. A couple, for instance, can start out in a duplex and live in one part while renting out the other apartment to pay off the mortgage. In addition, there are various income tax exemptions on investments of this sort.

For life insurance protection, the father or wage

earner should get convertible term insurance, the cheapest kind of insurance with the most benefit. A medical insurance plan is also a necessity for protection. Insurance is a poor way to invest money.

Before investing in stocks, the investor should check the following important guidelines in *The Standard and Poor Stock Guide* or a similar source of stock information. Most mutual funds are very poor investments.

1. Is it A rated or better?

2. Has it paid dividends for the last 30 years or more?

3. Is the yield on the stock at the buying price at least ten percent or more?

4. The stock should be bought when it is in the lowest 50 percent of its high-low cycle and sold when it gets up into its highest 50 percent. Investors try to determine the approximate low and high of the market to be certain of the time to sell and buy.

5. The Dow Jones Industrial average should be monitored to find out the highs and lows of the market. When the discount rate and prime rate trend starts going up (evidenced by three consecutive increases) investors generally sell their stock. They start buying when the discount rate has reached a high and has started downward (evidenced by three consecutive decreases).

6. A broker should know his clients' rules for investment to give them suggestions in line with their investment criteria.

The above rules make stocks an investment instead of a gamble. Finally, a Christian shouldn't buy any stock in a company which deals in tobacco, liquor, or other obviously objectionable elements.

Principle 6: Balancing income and family unity. Approximately 50 percent of the mothers with children under the age of 18 work outside the home. This factor can have a devastating effect on the family's unity for numerous reasons. However, carefully considered part-time jobs for mothers and children can help rather than hinder the family. The typical paper route or lawn jobs (with the son investing in the lawn mower) or a spray painting outfit can start a boy in a small business and give Dad an opportunity to teach, guide, and manage his teenage son. Girls can start with babysitting, dog sitting, or house sitting services. They could also start a summer or after-school nursery service as long as the total number of children doesn't get above the level that brings it under state jurisdiction and local zoning ordinances. Mothers who have accounting skills can also do bookkeeping several hours daily for small firms. They could also prepare tax forms. If they have typing or shorthand skills, they may consider typing term papers, etc. This job is especially lucrative if they live near a university. Telephone surveys, phone book deliveries, and various sales distributorships (Avon, Amway, Sarah Coventry) will also let the mother be home most of the time or away only during the time the children are in school.

A mother who wants to run a small nursery gives her children playmates and herself an outlet for training other children in the Gospel. At the same time, she is earning extra income for the family.

Finances can be a trouble spot in a marriage; but

by proper planning, hard work by all, judicious saving and spending, and by trusting the Lord, money problems can be eliminated and finances can be a source of blessing and family unity.

CASE STUDY

One of my friends, after being saved about a year, went to our pastor for financial help. He had consolidated all of his debts into one $4500 loan at 12 percent interest. He was earning $112 weekly, but his bills and expenses amounted to about $190 per week. His plea to the pastor was, "Every week I'm sinking deeper and deeper; what can I do?"

The pastor took him through the tithing principle with emphasis on Proverbs 3:9, 10. The man replied, "Pastor, I can't give to God other people's money; it is rightly theirs." After going through Malachi 3:8-11, the pastor prayed, "God, can you prove yourself in this impossible case." My friend made a covenant with the Lord to follow Proverbs 3:9, 10.

Two weeks later he got a large early morning paper route; the whole family helped him. It took him 14 months to pay off his large debt. Now nine years later he has tripled his earlier salary and is living in a $60,000 home which he bought at the bottom of the recession for $28,000; he owes now only about $10,000 on the mortgage. He has one girl in college, and his standard of living is much improved.

Trusting God in financial matters increased his faith to the point where he has become a very fruitful worker on a bus route, in soulwinning, and on visitation. He continually praises God for His goodness and bountiful provision.

Appendix A—Bible Action Truths For Married Love and a Happy Family Life

I. Marriage is based on the character of the participants (Ephesians 5:14-19).
   A. A born-again Christian (Ephesians 5:14; John 3).
   B. A spirit-filled Christian (Ephesians 5:18, 19; Galatians 5:22, 23).
      Spiritual life affects married love and married love affects the spiritual life.
      Married love is a perfect example of the believer's relationship with Christ.

II. Love: an unselfish or self-sacrificing desire to meet the needs of the cherished object. A mental attitude. I Corinthians 13:4-7, 11—childish to mature, holy love.
   A. Involves:
      1. Understanding the partner's needs (Proverbs 17:27; 14:1).
         a. Women: security and homemaking.
         b. Men: ego and physical (food and love).
      2. Giving: The circle of love (II Corinthians 9:6-8; Luke 6:38).

If children don't learn to love at home, they find it very hard to love people.

B. Love is:

> Spiritual
> Mental & Emotional
> Physical
> Tender telling
> Loving in little things
> Care in your contact

III. Communication: Ephesians 4:22-32

5 rules:
v. 25	Be open and honest.
v. 26-27	Talk up instead of blow up or clam up.
v. 28	Be industrious. Take full share of responsibilities.
v. 29	Edify by what and how you speak.
v. 30-32	Forgive with kind, tender-hearted spirit, I Corinthians 13:4.

IV. Rejoice and give thanks in everything (Ephesians 5:19, 20; I Thessalonians 5:18).

What for? (Romans 8:28; John 10:10) Are you enjoying the abundant life?

How? (Psalm 107:8) Praise the Lord seven times a day (Psalm 119:164).

V. Duty of the wife: submission and obedience—loses freedom but gains the benefits of security and protection (Ephesians 5:22-24).

A. Ephesians 5:22-24—God's rank of authority.

B. I Peter 3:1-6—To develop inner beauty; meek and quiet spirit.

I Timothy 2:9, 10—Modest and discreet with

good works.
Titus 2:4, 5—Obey: teach to be obedient
I Corinthians 14:34—Keep silent in church—
be obedient.
C. I Timothy 2:11-15—Woman is weaker—
was deceived.
D. I Corinthians 11:3, 7-12—Woman was
created for the man.
E. Genesis 3:16—Result of God's curse—rule
over thee.
F. Checklist for wives:
1. Are you submissive and obedient?
2. Do you have inner beauty?
3. Will you pray for your husband every
day?

VI. Duty of the husband: love and leadership—
husbands love your wives (Ephesians 5:25-29).
A. As Christ loved the church. As you love your
own body.
B. Don't be bitter against them (Colossians 3:19;
Proverbs 18:22).
Ephesians 4:26-27, 31
Anger—I Corinthians 14:20
C. Bitterness:
1. Creates negative mental attitudes resulting
in bickering and belittling.
2. Interrupts communication—indifference.
3. Kills warm emotional feelings—coldness.
D. Love, meeting the needs of his wife (affection
and security), keeps the husband from being
dictatorial (I Peter 3:7).
E. Checklist for husbands:
1. Do you tear down instead of build up your

wife?

2. Do you disagree with your wife's discipline of children?
3. Do you buy and use the car without her knowledge?
4. Do you make your wife beg for money?
5. Do you plan the family vacation yourself?

F. It takes two to make a marriage and two to break a marriage.

VII. One flesh—the physical relationship (Ephesians 5:31-33).

Ephesians 5:31—leave father and mother—family interference breaks up marriage.

Join or cleave—glued together (Greek)

Matthew 19:5, 6; Mark 10:6-8

Genesis 2:24—"one" same Hebrew word used in Deuteronomy 6:4.

Note the contrast in A, B, and C below: In marriage, ONLY the one-flesh relationship is God-ordained and honorable. God hates sex outside of marriage—fornication and adultery.

A. Hebrews 13:4—Honorable, bed undefiled.

Puritan view—pleasure and pleasing of the senses was denied.

Psalm 51:5—Does not teach the physical relationship as sin.

Hebrew parallelism of vs. 2, 3, 7—sin nature passes on at conception.

B. Proverbs 5:15-23—Rejoice with the wife of thy youth. Be satisfied and ravished with her love. Proverbs 18:22—Obtains favor with the Lord.

C. Frequency—I Corinthians 7:1-5

To avoid fornication.

Get married and give love to the marriage partner (vs. 2, 3).

Don't live unto yourself (vs. 4). Meet your partner's needs.

Don't defraud or rob the partner of what is rightfully his (vs. 5).

> Exception: With mutual consent, for a time to fast and pray. Come together again so Satan will not tempt.

The physical communication of married love becomes mechanical and animal unless the spiritual and psychological communication is first emphasized! Warning: Keep the marriage boundary. With feelings, the line between the spiritual, emotional, and physical is very thin.

D. Children are desirable (Psalm 127:3-5; 128:3). Don't judge others on the number of children they have.

Childless couples—let God answer your prayers (Matthew 21:22).

VIII. Children obey your parents (Ephesians 6:1-3; I Timothy 6:1-6)

A. First commandment with promise (Exodus 20:12).

1. Colossians 3:20—pleasing to the Lord.

2. John 14:21—shows love.

B. The remedy for disobedience.

1. Under the law—Exodus 21:15, 17; Deuteronomy 21:18-21.

2. Under grace, chasten—Hebrews 12:7-9; Proverbs 19:18.

3. How? With a rod—Proverbs 23:13, 14; 22:15; 13:24; 3:11-12.

IX. Fathers train your children (Ephesians 6:4; Joshua 24:14-24).

Represents law and order; God image. *Time-Testimony-Training:*

Salvation, Study the Word, Separation, Surrender, Soulwinning.

A. Proverbs 22:6—Teach by creed and deed. Who is teaching your children: TV? Ungodly schools? Playmates?

B. Isaiah 28:10—Line upon line, precept upon precept.

C. Proverbs 4:1, 2—Hear the father; gives good doctrine.

Proverbs 8:13—the fear of the Lord; 1:8 beginning of knowledge; and 9:10 wisdom.

D. Deuteronomy 6:6,7; II Timothy 1:5—Family altar.

The Supreme Court decision ruled prayer and Bible Study out of the public schools. Father's neglect rules them out of the home.

Appendix B—
Teaching Bible Action Truths

More and more Christians in these days are seeking to give their children a truly Christian education. Our purpose, of course, is to train leaders with sound Christian character to do the Lord's work and to glorify His name. Therefore, our children must learn to attain God's goals by applying biblical principles; when they act consistently in line with Bible truths, they will have Christian character.

We do not train Christian leaders with character merely by teaching them 10,000 facts in 12 years. Character can improve only as teachers identify strengths and weaknesses and teach their students to grasp fundamental Bible principles upon which to base their actions. Bible principles provide solid, absolute beliefs for daily actions.

Great Christian teachers know how to teach Bible truths in principle form and how to integrate all other material with this truth. Unfortunately, many Christian schools lack principled instruction based on the Bible's guidelines for action. Many students coming from Christian schools have been taught a lot of secular knowledge with Bible classes and chapel added; but they do not know basic Bible principles, and they do not know how to integrate knowledge with these principles. The 37 Bible Action Truths following are suggested as foundations for principled teaching, and are conveniently classified under eight action-reaction headings.

There are thousands of Bible action truths; those listed are the ones most directly affecting character. These principles can be used as the foundation for a Bible curriculum in a Christian school, a Sunday school, or a youth organization. They are also foundation stones upon which the entire Christian school curriculum and classroom teaching should be established. Not all of these principles can be integrated with every single subject, but they should become essential ingredients of the total Christian curriculum.

A balance in using these principles is important. It is easy to overemphasize one or two Bible truths above all others, thus causing our reaction to be warped and maladjusted. There are many different ways of teaching these truths and of integrating them into the curriculum. The proper utilization of Bible action truths will enrich the learning of the student and lead to a useful, balanced, and well-adjusted Christian life.

Of course, these principles are intended for the young person who has been born again and who is being taught the important doctrines of the Faith. Many Bible principles can be used by unsaved people, and they will work because their effectiveness depends on God's power and promise rather than man's condition. But an unregenerate man or woman is not inclined to follow Bible principles because he does not have the fear of the Lord (Proverbs 8:13) and because he does not really understand Bible truth (I Corinthians 2:14). Salvation brings the fear of the Lord, which is the beginning of wisdom and knowledge (Proverbs 1:7; 9:10).

True Christian education points children to the Bible, the absolute guide for living; it teaches them the principles in this guide, and it helps them learn how to implement these principles. Young people need to grasp Bible principles and make them part of their lives.

Christian schools do not exist for the purpose of building a church, a football team, or an academic record; success in these areas does not measure the Christian education of the school. Real success can be measured only by the number of graduates successfully serving the Lord, actively practicing Bible principles in their daily lives. Admittedly, the school cannot accomplish its task without the cooperation of the home and the church. All three must work together to build character in the child. The goal is a high one; but when home, church, and school work together in a systematic way, that goal can be reached.

Bible Action Truths

Man ought to react to God's actions by putting into practice the principles of the Word of God. Christian character is developed by learning Bible truths and putting them into action. The Bible Action Truths listed below are conveniently grouped into eight action-reaction categories. The first word indicates God's action, and the second word indi-

cates man's reaction. A careful study of the Bible
Action Truths and the accompanying Scriptures
listed below will assist you in understanding how
God wants you to act and react in this world.

Salvation-Separation

Salvation results from God's direct action. Although
man is unable to work for this "gift of God," the
Christian's reaction to salvation should be to separate himself from the world unto God.

Understanding Jesus Christ—Matthew 3:17; 16:16;
I Corinthians 15:3-4; Philippians 2:9-11

Repentance and faith—Luke 13:3; Isaiah 55:7; Acts
5:30-31; Hebrews 11:6; Acts 16:31

Separation from the world—John 17:6, 11, 14, 18;
II Corinthians 6:14-18; I John 2:15-16; James 4:4;
Romans 16:17-18; II John 10-11

Sonship-Servant

Only by an act of God the Father could sinful man
become a son of God. As a son of God, however, the
Christian must realize that he has been "bought
with a price"; he is now Christ's servant.

Authority—Romans   13:1-7;   I Peter   2:13-19;
I Timothy 6:1-5; Hebrews 13:17; Matthew 22:21;
I Thessalonians 5:12-13

Servanthood—Philippians 2:7-8; Ephesians 6:5-8

Faithfulness—I Corinthians 4:2; Matthew 25:23;
Luke 9:62

Goal setting—Proverbs 13:12, 19; Philippians 3:13;
Colossians 3:2; I Corinthians 9:24

Work—Ephesians 4:28; II Thessalonians 3:10-12

Enthusiasm—Colossians 3:23; Romans 12:11

Uniqueness-Unity

No one is a *mere person;* God has created each individual a unique being. But because God has an overall plan for His creation, each unique member must contribute to the unity of the entire body.

Self-concept—Psalm 139; Psalm 8:3-8; II Corinthians 5:17; Ephesians 2:10; 4:1-3, 11-13; II Peter 1:10

Mind—Philippians 2:5; 4:8; II Corinthians 10:5; Proverbs 23:7; Luke 6:45; Proverbs 4:23; Romans 7:23, 25; Daniel 1:8; James 1:8

Emotional control—Galatians 5:24; Proverbs 16:32; 25:28; II Timothy 1:7; Acts 20:24

Body as a temple—I Corinthians 6:19-20; 3:16-17

Unity of Christ and the Church—John 17:21; Ephesians 2:19-22; 5:23-32; II Thessalonians 3:6, 14, 15

Holiness-Habit

Believers are declared holy as a result of Christ's finished action on the cross. Daily holiness of life, however, comes from forming godly habits. A Christian must consciously establish godly patterns of action; he must develop habits of holiness.

Sowing and reaping—Galatians 6:7-8; Hosea 8:7; Matthew 6:1-8

Purity—I Thessalonians 4:1-7; I Peter 1:22

Honesty—II Corinthians 8:21; Romans 12:17; Proverbs 16:8; Ephesians 4:25

Victory—I Corinthians 10:13; Romans 8:37; I John 5:4; John 16:33; I Corinthians 15:57-58

Love-Life

We love God because He first loved us. God's action of manifesting His love to us through His Son demonstrates the truth that love must be exercised. Since God acted in love toward us, believers must act likewise by showing godly love to others.

Love—I John 3:11, 16-18; 4:7-21; Ephesians 5:2; I Corinthians 13; John 15:17

Giving—II Corinthians 9:6-8; Proverbs 3:9-10; Luke 6:8

Evangelism and missions—Psalm 126:5-6; Matthew 28:18-20; Romans 1:16-17; II Corinthians 5:11-21

Communication—Ephesians 4:22-29; Colossians 4:6; James 3:2-13; Isaiah 50:4

Friendliness—Proverbs 18:24; 17:17; Psalm 119:63

Communion-Consecration

Because sin separates man from God, any communion between man and God must be achieved by God's direct action of removing sin. Once communion is established, the believer's reaction should be to maintain a consciousness of this fellowship by living a consecrated life.

Bible study—I Peter 2:2-3; II Timothy 2:15; Psalm 119

Prayer—I Chronicles 16:11; I Thessalonians 5:17; John 15:7, 16; 16:24; Psalm 145:18; Romans 8:26-27

Spirit-filled—Ephesians 5:18-19; Galatians 5:16, 22-23; Romans 8:13-14; I John 1:7-9

Clear conscience—I Timothy 1:19; Acts 24:16

Forgiveness—Ephesians 4:30-32; Luke 17:3-4; Colossians 3:13; Matthew 18:15-17; Mark 11:25-26

Grace-Gratitude

Grace is unmerited favor. Man does not deserve God's grace. However, after God bestows His grace, believers should react with an overflow of gratitude.

Grace—I Corinthians 15:10; Ephesians 2:8-9

Exaltation of Christ—Colossians 1:12-21; Ephesians 1:17-23; Philippians 2:9-11; Galatians 6:14; Hebrews 1:2-3; John 1:1-4, 14; 5:23

Praise—Psalm 107:8; Hebrews 13:15; I Peter 2:9; Ephesians 1:6; I Chronicles 16:23-36; 29:11-13

Contentment—Philippians 4:11; I Timothy 6:6-8; Psalm 77:3; Proverbs 15:16; Hebrews 13:5

Humility—I Peter 5:5-6; Philippians 2:3-4

Power-Prevailing

Believers can prevail only as God gives the power. "I can do all things *through Christ*." God is the source of our power used in fighting the good fight of faith.

Faith in God's promises—II Peter 1:4; Philippians 4:6; Romans 4:16-21; I Thessalonians 5:18; Romans 8:28; I Peter 5:7; Hebrews 3:18—4:11

Faith in the power of the Word of God—Hebrews 4:12; Jeremiah 23:29; Psalm 119; I Peter 1:23-25

Fight—Ephesians 6:11-17; II Timothy 4:7-8; I Timothy 6:12; I Peter 5:8-9

Courage—I Chronicles 28:20; Joshua 1:9; Hebrews 13:6; Ephesians 3:11-12; Acts 4:13, 31

The 4M Formula (from Psalm 119)

1) Mark these Bible action truths during your Scripture reading (verse 9).

2) Memorize the verses which best represent the truths (verse 11).

3) Meditate on the verses throughout the day (verse 15).

4) Master these Bible action truths in your daily life until they master you (verse 17).

Appendix C—Bible ABC's

The Scriptures counsel new Christians to desire the sincere milk of the Word. *"As newborn babes, desire the sincere milk of the word, that ye may grow thereby, If so be ye have tasted that the Lord is gracious;" I Peter 2:2, 3.* Christian parents need to help their children learn simple Bible verses that can be put into action in their lives so they will accept the Lord early in life and grow strong spiritually. These verses are categorized under the ABC's so the children can learn the alphabet while they are learning important verses. The following are verses of doctrine and action. Help your children to apply these verses in everyday situations.

A
Ask, and it shall be given you. Luke 11:9. Also, Isaiah 53:6; Romans 3:10; Romans 3:23; I Thessalonians 5:22

B
Be ye kind one to another. Ephesians 4:32. Also, Acts 16:31; Acts 23:11; Romans 12:10; James 1:22

C
Children obey your parents in the Lord: for this is right.

Ephesians 6:1. Also, Psalm 37:5; Psalm 37:8; Isaiah 40:1

D

Do all things without murmurings and disputings. Philippians 2:14. Also, Psalm 34:14; Psalm 37:4; Proverbs 12:20a; Proverbs 13:19

E

Even a child is known by his doings. Proverbs 20:11. Also, Proverbs 15:3; I Corinthians 15:33; James 1:17

F

Fret not thyself. Psalm 37:1. Also, Isaiah 43:5; John 3:16; Ephesians 2:8

G

God loveth a cheerful giver. II Corinthians 9:7b. Also, Psalm 112:5a; Proverbs 12:25b; Proverbs 14:7a; Isaiah 39:8; Ephesians 6:2

H

Hear ye children, the instruction of a father. Proverbs 4:1. Also, Proverbs 3:9; Proverbs 4:10; Proverbs 10:5; Isaiah 6:8b; Ephesians 6:2

I

In everything give thanks. I Thessalonians 5:18. Also, Genesis 1:1; John 13:17; Philippians 4:13; Hebrews 13:6b; James 1:5; I John 1:9

J

Jesus said unto him, "I am the way, the truth and the life." John 14:6. Also, Psalm 30:5b

K

Keep thy tongue from evil. Psalm 34:13. Also, Exodus 23:7; Psalm 19:13a; Proverbs 4:23; Proverbs 7:2; Ecclesiastes 5:1

L

Love one another. I John 3:11b. Also, Proverbs 12:22; Matthew 6:19a; Luke 6:27b; I Corinthians 16:2b; I Corinthians 16:14; Ephesians 4:29, 31

M

Make a joyful noise unto the Lord. Psalm 100:1. Also, Proverbs 6:20; Proverbs 15:13; Proverbs 17:22; Philippians 4:19; James 5:7

N

Neither shalt thou profane the name of God. Leviticus 18:21. Also, Matthew 5:15; Romans 9:20; I Corinthians 10:10; II Thessalonians 3:8, 10b

O

Overcome evil with good. Romans 12:21b. Also, I Samuel 15:22b; I Chronicles 16:34; Psalm 118:1; Jeremiah 7:23; Romans 13:8; Hebrews 13:17

P

Pray one for another. James 5:16b. Also Proverbs 16:24; I Thessalonians 5:17; II Timothy 4:2a

Q

Quench not the spirit. I Thessalonians 5:19. Also, Psalm 119:154; I Corinthians 16:13b-14

R

Rest in the Lord. Psalm 37:7. Also, Romans 12:15; Romans 12:17; Ephesians 5:16

S

Seven times a day do I praise thee. Psalm 119:164. Also, I Chronicles 16:23; Proverbs 15:1; Ephesians 4:25b; Ephesians 5:19; I Thessalonians 4:11b; II Timothy 2:15

T

Trust in the Lord with all thine heart. Proverbs 3:5. Also, Ecclesiastes 3:1; John 3:15; Philippians 4:8b-9a

U

Use hospitality. I Peter 4:9. Also, Proverbs 16:22a

V

Vengeance is mine; I will repay, saith the Lord. Romans 12:19. Also, Ecclesiastes 12:8; John 3:3b

W

Whatsoever ye do, do it heartily as to the Lord. Colossians 3:23. Also, Ecclesiastes 9:10; Psalm 37:34; Psalm 62:5; Matthew 26:41; I Corinthians 3:9; I Thessalonians 4:11b

X

eXalt the Lord, our God. Psalm 99:9. Also, John 3:3

Y

Ye are the light of the world. Matthew 5:15. Also II Chronicles 30:8b; Proverbs 4:1; Isaiah 49:15b

Z

Zacchaeus, make haste. Luke 19:5. Also, Numbers 25:13b

Use the printed out verses for the very young child; add verses and all of a verse as the child gets older.

Appendix D—Discipline of Children

DISCIPLINE

Training: Teaching and guiding children to recognize and respect the boundary lines of any situation.

Control: Provide the right conditions for right action.

Correction: Providing remedial action when children go beyond the boundary lines.

Training—Proverbs 22:6

Make boundary lines definite but general.

Boundary lines should expand as children grow older.

Set limits or boundary lines—"Limits bring security and create a frame of reference for life within which a child can work and play at his best." Expect a child to test these limits.

Parents should agree on training. Keep the father in the proper perspective.

Do not moralize unless willing as parents to set the example. Teach by deed as well as by creed.

Do not expect perfection or set too high of standards or goals for your child.

Keep communication routes open. Explain and discuss rules. (Who likes to follow all rules blindly?)

Control—Some common causes of behavior and methods for dealing with them: Behavior is caused! If possible, remove the cause, make provision for it; or counteract the effects.

The sin nature of man, producing the works of the flesh. A well-ordered environment with firm boundary lines. Be filled with the Spirit, manifest love and pray for your child.

The simple, uncomplicated desire to attract attention. Give them time and attention in acceptable ways.

Feels lack of self-control. He is not mature emotionally.

Individual differences. Know the learning level and skill level of your child. He may not be resourceful alone or he may be trying to help, or he may be very curious.

Dynamic energy: Direct energy into profitable channels. He may be bored.

Poor child-rearing techniques. Prepare yourself by reading materials and basing methods in light of the Word.

Subtle and hidden causes such as poor home conditions or the physical and emotional aspects of the child not considered.

Distraction and substitution.

Types of Correction—Remedial Action Timing is important. Do it calmly and not in anger, show love and pray with the child; sometimes he needs an explanation. After the punishment, FORGET it! (Proverbs 3:11, 12)

Verbal (Proverbs 29:17—tongue lashing)
Withholding of privilege, object, etc.
Consequences
Physical (Proverbs 23:13—corporal punishment)
Isolation

General Principles

Respect a child as an individual who has some rights.

The child is a social being; he is not just a small adult.

Carry out promises and threats; otherwise, do not make them. Be consistent in daily living.

Be positive in rules and commands when possible.

Be flexible, use imagination. Avoid the "letter of the law." Rules are made to help us—we control the rules rather than the rules controlling us. Too much rigidity by adults shows insecurity and lack of maturity.

Teach responsibility, sprinkle criticism with praise; show the child how to improve; at times accept imperfection and do not compare with others.